ADAMS

ELECTRONIC
JOB SEARCH
ALMANAC 1998

Top career publications from Adams Media Corporation

Other Adams Almanacs:

The Adams Businesses You Can Start
Almanac ($10.95)
The Adams Cover Letter Almanac
($10.95)
The Adams Job Interview Almanac
($12.95)
The Adams Jobs Almanac, 1998 ($15.95)
The Adams Resume Almanac ($10.95)

Other Career Titles:

America's Fastest Growing Employers,
2nd Ed. ($16.00)
Career Shifting ($9.95)
Cold Calling Techniques, 3rd Ed. ($7.95)
The Complete Resume & Job Search Book
for College Students ($10.95)
Cover Letters That Knock 'em Dead, 3rd
Ed. ($10.95)
Every Woman's Essential Job Hunting &
Resume Book ($10.95)
The Harvard Guide to Careers in the Mass
Media ($7.95)
High Impact Telephone Networking for
Job Hunters ($6.95)
How to Become Successfully Self-
Employed, 2nd Ed. ($9.95)
How to Get a Job in Education, 2nd Ed.
($15.95)
The Job Hunter's Checklist ($5.95)
The Job Search Handbook ($6.95)
Knock 'em Dead, 1998 ($12.95)
The Lifetime Career Manager ($20.00 hc)
The MBA Advantage ($12.95)
The Minority Career Book ($9.95)
The National Jobline Directory ($7.95)
The New Rules of the Job Search Game
($10.95)
Outplace Yourself ($15.95)
Over 40 and Looking for Work? ($7.95)
Reengineering Yourself ($12.95)
The Resume Handbook, 3rd Ed. ($7.95)
Resumes That Knock 'em Dead, 3rd Ed.
($10.95)
Richard Beatty's Job Search Networking
($9.95)
300 New Ways to Get a Better Job ($7.95)

The JobBank Series:
each JobBank book is $16.95

The Atlanta JobBank, 1998
The Austin/San Antonio JobBank, 1st Ed.
The Boston JobBank, 1998
The Carolina JobBank, 4th Ed.
The Chicago JobBank, 1998
The Cincinnati JobBank, 1st Ed.
The Cleveland JobBank, 1st Ed.
The Dallas-Fort Worth JobBank, 1998
The Denver JobBank, 9th Ed.
The Detroit JobBank, 7th Ed.
The Florida JobBank, 1998
The Houston JobBank, 1998
The Indianapolis JobBank, 1st Ed.
The Las Vegas JobBank, 1st Ed.
The Los Angeles JobBank, 1998
The Minneapolis-St. Paul JobBank, 10th Ed.
The Missouri JobBank, 1st Ed.
The Northern New England JobBank, 1st Ed.
The New Mexico JobBank, 1st Ed.
The Metropolitan New York JobBank,
1998
The Upstate New York JobBank, 1st Ed.
The Greater Philadelphia JobBank, 1998
The Phoenix JobBank, 6th Ed.
The Pittsburgh JobBank, 1st Ed.
The Portland JobBank, 1st Ed.
The Salt Lake City JobBank, 1st Ed.
The San Francisco Bay Area JobBank, 1998
The Seattle JobBank, 1998
The Tennessee JobBank, 3rd Ed.
The Virginia JobBank, 1st Ed.
The Metropolitan Washington DC
JobBank, 1998
The Wisconsin JobBank, 1st Ed.

The JobBank Guide to Computer & High-
Tech Companies ($16.95)

The National JobBank, 1998
(Covers entire U.S.: $320.00 hc)

The JobBank Guide to Employment
Services, 1998-1999
(Covers entire U.S.: $199.00 hc)

Adams JobBank FastResume Suite
(CD-ROM, call for details)

ADAMS

ELECTRONIC JOB SEARCH ALMANAC 1998

Adams Media Corporation
Holbrook, Massachusetts

Credits

Steven Graber, *Managing Editor*
Andy Richardson, *Editor*
Emily E. Ehrenstein, *Writer/Researcher*
Todd A. Donatello, *Editorial Intern*

Published by Adams Media Corporation
260 Center Street, Holbrook, Massachusetts 02343

ISBN: 1-55850-753-1
Manufactured in Canada.

J I H G F E D C B A

Product or brand names used in this book may be trademarks or registered trademarks. Any use of these names does not convey endorsement by or other affiliation with the name holder.

Adams Media Corporation is a publisher of career books and software products, including CareerCity, a career-related site on the World Wide Web. While the publisher is a potential competitor with many of the services and products listed in this book, every effort has been made to ensure editorial objectivity and impartiality.

Every effort has been made to ensure that all material in this book is current as of the time of this writing. However, due to the nature of the technologies discussed here, this information is subject to change. Readers should check with the individual services and products to find up-to-date information, such as current prices, fees, and features.

This publication is designed to provide accurate and authoritative information with regard to the subject matter covered. It is sold with the understanding that the publisher is not engaged in rendering legal, accounting, or other professional advice. If legal advice or other expert assistance is required, the services of a qualified professional person should be sought.
— From a *Declaration of Principles* jointly adopted by a Committee of the American Bar Association and a Committee of Publishers and Associations.

This book is available at quantity discounts for bulk purchases.
For more information, call 1-800-872-5627 (in Massachusetts 781-767-8100).

Visit our home page at http://www.careercity.com

CONTENTS

How to Use This Book **11**

Introduction: Job Hunting in the Electronic Age **15**

Part I
Reinventing the Traditional Resume

1. Your Electronic Resume **29**
The essential elements of an effective electronic resume. Includes information on electronic resume databases.

2. Posting Your Resume Online **51**
The advantages of posting your resume to an online database, as well as a step-by-step guide to preparing your resume for posting. This chapter also tells you where to post your resume.

3. Video and Multimedia Resumes **75**
How to determine if an unconventional resume is right for you, and how to use these media effectively.

Part II
Finding Advertised Jobs the Electronic Way

4. Commercial Online Services **87**
Learn where the jobs are on America Online, CompuServe, Delphi, GEnie, The Microsoft Network, and Prodigy.

5. Usenet Newsgroups **115**
Discover more than 90,000 job listings in 100 of the best newsgroups.

6. The World Wide Web 133
A brief history of the Web and forty-five outstanding resources for hundreds of thousands of job listings, career advice, and more.

7. Gopher and Telnet 187
Five excellent resources from the Internet's smallest jewels.

8. Bulletin Board Systems 197
The simplest way to get online. Use BBSs to find job listings and other employment information.

9. Company Joblines 201
Discover one of the best-kept secrets in job hunting. Includes a selection of joblines.

Part III
Tapping the Hidden Job Market

10. Electronic Employer Databases 209
Use company directories on CD-ROM to create a target list of employers, and find valuable company information in business periodical databases.

11. Researching Companies Online 223
The best places to find company information online, including where to find business databases on the World Wide Web and commercial online services, and how to locate a company's home page on the Web.

12. Networking Online 243
Electronic discussion groups on Usenet and commercial online services. Learn the ins and outs of "netiquette" in order to communicate effectively in cyberspace.

Part IV
Other Advances in Electronic Job Hunting

13. Computer-Assisted Job Interviews 263
Learn why you might meet with a computer at your next job interview, and what the computer tells the company about you.

14. Computerized Assessment Tests **275**
Why many companies use skills, personality, and integrity tests,
and what you should expect if you're asked to take one.

15. Job Hunting and Career Management Software . . .**281**
Resume writing and interview preparation programs that can help
you organize an efficient job search.

Glossary of Terms **291**

Index **299**

ACKNOWLEDGMENTS

A special thanks goes to Bill Duffy for all of his technical assistance and for answering so many questions so patiently. An additional thanks goes to Kenny Brooks, for helpful suggestions and information during production of the first edition of this book, and Chris Maligno, for similar input during the second. And finally, a hearty thank you to Sue Beale, without whose efforts the book you're holding would have been far less graphically pleasing.

Thanks also to Kerstin Bagus, Pinkerton Security and Investigation Services; Even Brande, Aspen Tree Software; Vera Ehmann, Career Advantage; and Karen McGreal, Restrac, Inc.

HOW TO USE THIS BOOK

The *Adams Electronic Job Search Almanac 1998* is designed to prepare job hunters for the information age. In it, you will find hundreds of electronic resources to help with every aspect of your job hunt, from writing your resume and finding job openings to preparing for job interviews. Regardless of your level of experience with technology, you will find an abundance of valuable information within these pages.

You can approach this book in two different ways. One option is to read it cover to cover so that you learn about the full spectrum of electronic job hunting. Or, you can use it as a handy reference guide in order to find resources of particular interest, such as the Web address for a job hunting site that specializes in entry-level jobs.

In our **Introduction**, we introduce you to the concept of electronic job hunting. This includes a discussion of *why* it's important to keep up with changing technology, and an overview of how to get started with your electronic job hunt—including purchasing hardware and software, setting up, and strategies to follow.

You may decide to begin your electronic job hunt by creating an electronic resume. In **Part One, Reinventing the Traditional Resume**, you'll learn why you should have one, and where to distribute it in order to maximize your exposure. We also tell you about video and multimedia resumes, two types of electronic resumes that are sure to make you stand out with employers.

But if you simply want to know where to find job listings online, turn to **Part Two, Finding Advertised Jobs the Electronic Way**. In this section, we tell you about the *best* places to look for jobs. You'll discover where to find thousands of job listings online through the World Wide Web, commercial online services, Usenet, recorded joblines, and more.

You'll also learn how to create a target list of potential employers, and where to uncover valuable company information that you can use during your interview. And if you're interested in finding the best online discussion groups for meeting and chatting with other professionals in your field, turn to our chapter on networking. You'll find all this information and more in **Part Three, Tapping the Hidden Job Market**.

Finally, **Part Four, Other Advances in Electronic Job Hunting**, covers other aspects of electronic job hunting, including commercial career and job-search software products, and what to do if you're told you'll talk to a computer, instead of a person, at your next job interview.

About the Update

Keep in mind that in this age of rapidly changing technology, electronic resources are coming and going faster than you can say "information superhighway," so Web sites, electronic databases, and other services described here may have changed since the time of this writing. Since publication of the 1997 edition of this book, we have watched while once powerful companies and services have all but disappeared, and new players have emerged to take their share of the marketplace. In the book's largest section, on World Wide Web job hunting sites, we have added nearly two dozen new resources, while saying goodbye to several others.

We have made our best efforts to ensure that the information in this book is as accurate and up-to-date as possible, verifying every shred of information from the last edition and adding new material where appropriate. That said, there is little doubt that some changes will occur even in the time it takes for this book to be printed, and information, particularly concerning prices, should be used more as a guideline than as gospel.

One Final Note

We recommend using the resources described in this book as a complement to your other job hunting methods. In other words, don't stop doing what has given you success in the past. Not everyone will want to, or should, use *all* the services mentioned. Instead, this book will help you determine which resources best meet *your* job hunting needs, so that you can start down the road to career success!

JOB HUNTING
IN THE
ELECTRONIC AGE

Looking for a new job in today's economy can be quite diffi-cult, and often frustrating. Corporate downsizing and layoffs have flooded the job market with thousands of qualified and eager job candidates. And with the specter of budget cuts and unemploy-ment hanging over so many companies, job security has become a thing of the past. It is no surprise, then, that competition for available positions is intense. For instance, a single help-wanted advertisement in the Sunday newspaper often yields hundreds of resumes from suitable applicants!

Now this leads us to the questions plaguing all job hunters, regardless of their occupation or level of experience: How do I get ahead of the competition? Where can I find that winning edge that will land me a new job? Today, those answers often lie with technology.

New advances in technology have given job hunters hundreds of new resources to turn to. Electronic resume and employment databases, job hunting software, and the Internet are just some of the advances that have made it easier than ever before to write high-quality resumes, make industry contacts, and uncover unad-vertised job openings. And most experts agree that the ability to use these electronic resources effectively is becoming increasingly important in managing both an effective job hunt, and in the long run, your career.

The Electronic Revolution

Our society is in the middle of a revolution—a technological revolution that is radically changing the way we live. Just think back to twenty years ago—many of the conveniences we now take for granted, such as ATMs and VCRs, did not even exist!

This electronic revolution has had an enormous effect on the workplace. The use of personal computers, for instance, has tremendously boosted the productivity and efficiency of companies. Voice mail, fax machines, and more recently, email, have changed the way we communicate. Technology has created a global marketplace in which differences such as geography and language are no longer barriers for trade and communication.

A recent nationwide survey of corporations indicated that computer literacy and knowledge are the most important skills that managers look for when hiring new employees. This survey underscores the importance of technology in today's workplace. And for the job hunter, the message behind this survey is simple: If you fail to keep up, you may find yourself left behind.

Why Electronic Job Hunting?

Looking for a new job is rarely a pleasurable activity, but new advances in technology can help ease some of the stress normally associated with job hunting. With all the new resources available, relying on the Sunday newspaper or old college friends to find job leads is no longer necessary. Electronic job hunting opens a whole new avenue of contacts and opportunities—areas that were previously hidden or otherwise unavailable to the general public. The following are some additional reasons to add electronic resources to your job hunting arsenal:

- **As we mentioned earlier in this chapter, an under-standing and knowledge of computers is the most sought after skill in new employees.** Using electronic resources to find a job—even something as simple as emailing your resume to a company—is an easy way to demonstrate your computer skills to a potential employer. Any employer is sure to be impressed by anyone with the savvy and initiative to use this medium.

- **Submitting your resume to an electronic resume database or posting your resume online will put your skills on display** for the thousands of hiring managers and human resources professionals nationwide who regularly search these databases. This widespread exposure makes you a potential candidate for thousands of job openings that are *never* advertised. Plus, online discussion groups can help you form an international network of contacts in your field, which may be helpful when it comes time to look for a new job.

- **By using electronic business directories, either online or on CD-ROM, you can precisely identify those companies that hire employees in your field and with your background.** These databases also contain enough company information, such as press releases or financial statements, to give you a good indication of whether a particular company is right for you.

- **Not only are the Internet and commercial online services available to job hunters twenty-four hours a day, seven days a week,** but their national and international scopes are ideal for job hunters considering relocating to another city, state, or country.

- **Finally, you can find hundreds of thousands of job listings unavailable anywhere else** by using company recorded joblines and online job databases on Bulletin Board Systems, the Internet, and commercial online services. Not surprisingly, the huge collection of jobs available is the main reason most people turn to electronic job hunting.

Electronic vs. Online Job Hunting

Many people mistakenly believe that electronic job hunting is just another term for job hunting online. But that is not the case. Electronic job hunting means much more than simply logging on to the Internet and searching for job listings. Instead, **electronic job hunting means taking advantage of all the technological resources available** and using them to further your career.

Job hunters without online access may feel left out of the revolution, but in reality, there are still plenty of options available. For instance, a job hunter doesn't even need to own a computer in order to hear job announcements from a recorded employer jobline! Following are some more ideas to help you incorporate technology into your job search:

- **Write an electronic resume.** Having an electronic resume is virtually a necessity in today's job market. An electronic resume is simply a resume that is stripped of special formatting, making it easy for a computer to read. Once you prepare an electronic resume, you can submit it to an electronic resume database, or simply mail it out to your target employers. Many companies now have applicant tracking systems, which means that resumes are automatically entered into an in-house resume database that is searched whenever there's a job opening.

- **Create a video or multimedia resume.** A video resume can almost be compared to a video interview, with the candidate describing his or her qualifications in front of a camera. A multimedia resume is one that uses text, sound, and graphics to relate your qualifications, and is usually mailed to a company on a floppy disk. Sending a video or multimedia resume to an employer is a surefire way to make you stand out from the crowd, but at the same time, it is really only appropriate if you're in a creative or highly technical field.

- **Take advantage of company joblines.** As mentioned earlier, recorded joblines are one of the best ways to find out about the job openings at a particular company. Joblines are phone lines maintained by a company specifically for the purpose of announcing job openings. You can also generally find out application and employment information—such as typical benefits offered—through these joblines.

- **Research employers through commercial business databases.** Developing a target list of potential employers and researching a company in-depth for a job interview have become much simpler, thanks to electronic business databases like *Hoover's Handbook*. Once available only as print directories, *Hoover's Handbook* and other similar resources now come in CD-ROM or diskette versions, which makes them much easier (and faster) to search for specific information.

- **Use job hunting software.** Programs such as Adams JobBank FastResume Suite and WinWay Resume offer a variety of electronic job hunting assistance. With the help of these and other programs, you can easily create a professional-quality resume and organize your contacts. You can also prepare for a job interview, often with a video interview tutorial, complete with sample questions and answers.

- **Prepare for computer-assisted job interviews and assessment tests.** With many companies, your first interview may well be with a computer, not a person. As impersonal as they sound, computer-assisted job interviews seem to be the wave of the future, especially in companies that hire large volumes of entry-level employees. Similarly, computerized assessment tests examine your skills, personality, and integrity in order to determine how well you will fit with a particular job. Together, these two programs attempt to raise the quality of employees and lower turnover by ensuring that the employee fits the job.

Job Hunting Resources Available Online

Job hunters with online access have an even greater selection of resources from which to choose. There are hundreds of services available that can help you with all aspects of the job hunt, including networking, researching companies, posting resumes, and—most importantly—finding job listings. Job hunting resources are found on both the Internet and commercial online services. Additionally, Bulletin Board Systems (BBSs), which represent a part of cyberspace that does not fall into either of these two areas, are also an excellent job hunting resource, particularly for job listings.

Commercial Online Services

These services, which charge users to access their resources, are more recognizable by their brand names: **America Online**, **CompuServe**, **The Microsoft Network**, and **Prodigy**. In general, they are excellent resources for networking and researching companies, although they also provide job listings. What's more, all these services provide their users with full access to the Internet and the vast employment resources available there. America Online (AOL) and CompuServe are the two largest commercial online services, and not surprisingly, they have the most resources to offer job hunters.

America Online is considered by many to have the strongest and largest collection of job listings available through a commercial online service. CompuServe, meanwhile, has dozens of high-quality professional discussion groups that are ideal for networking, as well as a number of searchable business databases that offer in-depth information on tens of thousands of companies, in both the United States and abroad. Microsoft has worked to get into the game through acquisitions and partnerships with various Internet software companies, and Prodigy also has several quality resources worth checking out. The smaller services—like Delphi and GEnie—lack the quantity of resources presently found on AOL or CompuServe. At the same time, these services do provide their somewhat smaller base of users with a number of career resources, including discussion groups, job listings, and employer databases. *For more information, including how to subscribe to a service, refer to Chapter 4, Commercial Online Services.*

The Internet

The Internet, or ARPANET as it was originally called, was developed in 1969 by the United States government, which wanted to create a communications system that could withstand a nuclear attack. But after the fall of the Berlin Wall in 1989, the perceived need for such a system ended, and the government began encouraging commercial use of the Internet. Thus, what was once the exclusive playground for academics and high-level government workers has grown into an international network of over 25 million users, with thousands more signing on every day.

There are four separate areas that are all part of the Internet: Gopher, Telnet, Usenet, and the World Wide Web. Together, these four areas represent the largest collection of job hunting information found online, including hundreds of thousands of job listings. It is no surprise, then, that when most people think of electronic job hunting, they think of the Internet.

- **Gopher.** Gopher is a menu-based system of organizing information on the Internet. It was also the first step in making the Internet more user-friendly, with its easy-to-manage menus and powerful search engines, Veronica and Jughead. Because it was developed at the University of Minnesota and quickly became a favorite of academics at other universities, Gopher remains an excellent source of academic and other specialized job listings. For example, it has one of the few employment resources found online that is dedicated to the arts.

- **Telnet.** Telnet is the smallest area of the Internet and getting smaller. Telnet is a good place to look for federal job listings and other information regarding applying for a federal job. Telnet is also useful as a way of connecting to other sites, such as a Gopher server.

- **Usenet.** The User's Network is comprised of more than 20,000 newsgroups, or electronic discussion groups, where people can exchange information, discuss ideas, or just chat. The very nature of Usenet makes it a natural for networking. With so many different newsgroups to choose from, you are sure to find one in your field of interest. Usenet also contains newsgroups dedicated to the posting of resumes and "situations wanted" messages, and is an *outstanding* resource for job listings, with over 100,000 offerings.

- **The World Wide Web.** Currently, the Web is probably the best known area of the Internet, due mainly to the phenomenal growth it has experienced within the past two years. The Web has dozens of excellent electronic career centers that offer all kinds of job hunting advice and information, including an ever-growing number of large databases of job listings. In fact, the Web has by far the largest collection of job listings found online.

A Word of Caution

While enough cannot be said regarding the benefits of electronic job hunting, it's important to continue using traditional job hunting methods, such as attending professional meetings, tapping into your network of contacts, and contacting employers directly. The rule of never relying on only one method to find a job extends to electronic job hunting.

At the same time, resources such as job hunting software and electronic business databases can actually help you with a traditional job search. For example, a resume writing program can help you write a lively, professional-quality resume that is sure to get you noticed, and an employer database on CD-ROM can help you locate potential employers, who you can then contact through traditional methods.

Currently, the hype surrounding the information superhighway somewhat outweighs its realities. While the Internet and commercial online services are continually improving and expanding their services, true commercialization of these services is still years away. One recent survey, which indicated that less than 20 percent of the United States population had even *heard* of the Internet, illustrates this point. As one expert said, "We are in the midst of an explosion, and the dust has yet to settle." Fortunately, career and jobs services is one area of cyberspace that is definitely living up to its promise.

Where to Begin

Now that you understand the benefits, as well as the limitations, of an electronic job hunt, you will need some basic equipment; namely, a computer, a modem, and an online or Internet service account. If you're a college or graduate student, you should have access through your college or university. Most schools now provide students with an Internet connection and an online account.

But if you're not a student and you don't already own a computer, you'll need to purchase the necessary hardware. Although more and more companies provide their employees with access to the Internet or a commercial online service, we strongly discourage you from using these resources at work, even after hours. It's not only a risky undertaking, but—because of the fee-based nature of the Internet and commercial services—borders on the unethical.

You have two choices of computers: a Macintosh or a PC-compatible machine. Macintoshes are much less common than PCs, and if you decide to buy one, you will have far fewer choices in terms of hardware, accessories, and software. A Macintosh with a System 8 operating system and a minimum of 16 MB memory is a solid choice. For a PC, buy a Pentium processor. Also, you'll need a Windows 3.1 or Windows 95 operating system, as well as at least 16 MB memory. A CD-ROM drive now comes standard on most new computers, and this will be necessary if you want to use the job hunting software that's discussed in Chapter 15.

As for modems, get the best and fastest modem that you can afford, which currently means either a 33,600 or 56,600 BPS modem. Anything slower, such as a 14,400 BPS modem, will drive up your phone bills, and using graphically rich services, such as the Web or America Online, will be painfully slow. With modems, quality matters as much, if not more, than speed. A high-quality modem has the ability to detect and correct errors in your phone line and connection.

Most new computers come with an internal modem already installed, but if you have an older computer that did not come with a modem, you'll need to purchase one. You can choose from either an internal or external modem. Most computer experts prefer internal modems, but then you'll have to disassemble your computer in order to install it, a prospect that does not exactly thrill the technically challenged among us.

You may want to consider an extra telephone line to connect to your modem. You can use your regular phone line, but you may, depending on your modem software, need to turn off any special features, such as call waiting, before you go online.

Once your modem and connection are working, you must decide whether you want to use a direct Internet connection or a commercial online service. (Remember, all commercial online services also provide full Internet access.) **Most newcomers choose a commercial online service, mainly because of the wide range of services offered and their ease of use.** You can subscribe to a service by installing the service's software, which is provided free of charge. You'll also commonly receive a free, one-month trial period. A commercial online service generally charges a flat monthly fee of about $10, which includes a set number of free hours each month. Additional hours cost about $2–$4 each. There are also deals for unlimited usage, usually in the $20 per month range. Such deals have become far more commonplace with the increasing popularity of the World Wide Web.

A direct Internet connection is generally the choice of experienced users, who are more inclined to know the subtleties and nuances of the Internet. You can buy Internet starter kits at a computer store, or look in the phone book for "Internet service providers" for instructions on how to sign up. In general, a direct Internet connection can cost as little as $10–$20 a month, often with an unlimited number of hours.

Online Strategies

Whether you chose a direct Internet connection or a commercial online service, take some time to become familiar with the service and the resources it offers. Check out some career areas, such as the big career centers on the Web. Lurk in a few discussion groups to get a sense of what they are really about. In addition to familiarizing yourself with a service, this process will also give you a good sense of how long it takes to find what you want online, so you'll be able to manage your time online better.

Try going online during off-peak hours, either early morning or late night. Services experience less traffic at these times, so it can be much easier to get through. And be sure that you are dialing into a local phone number. This will save you money on your phone bill.

It's also a good idea to know what you want to accomplish *before* you go online. Have an agenda prepared, complete with keywords to search for, or the names and addresses of sites you want to visit. Again, this will save you time and money because you won't be fumbling around online for the right keyword or address. Also, having a plan will lessen the chances that you'll get sidetracked into a discussion group dealing with such issues as who should be cast in the next *Batman* movie.

On the Web, use search engines such as Yahoo!, Excite, and Alta Vista to help you find what you need in less time. These powerful search engines can help you locate specific information and many will also search Usenet.

Don't rely on one particular area of the online world for all your job information. The World Wide Web is very glamorous, but don't forget those old reliables like Usenet newsgroups and Bulletin Board Systems, as well as offline options like joblines. After you spend some time exploring, you'll probably discover that certain resources work best for you. Narrow your efforts to those areas, since the more focus you have, the more effective your job search will be.

Finally, be patient. It takes time to learn about all the resources described here, and you may not see any results from your efforts for some time. And even if you end up finding a new job in a traditional way, such as through a friend or in the newspaper, you have still learned valuable skills that will help you throughout your career.

PART ONE

REINVENTING THE TRADITIONAL RESUME

CHAPTER ONE

YOUR ELECTRONIC RESUME

With companies slashing recruiting budgets and trimming hiring staffs, they rely increasingly on emerging technologies to find qualified candidates for job openings. Many companies use automated applicant tracking systems to process and sort employment applications. Other companies use the services of electronic employment database companies to fill specific openings. This means that your resume will be read by more computers and fewer people. **Your resume, therefore, must be in a format that is easy for a computer to recognize and understand**. Otherwise, your application may quickly begin collecting dust.

Basically, this is how it works: Once a company receives your resume, it is fed through a scanner, which sends an image of the document to a computer. The computer "reads" your resume, looking for keywords, and then files your resume accordingly in its database. When an employer has an opening to fill, he or she will search the database for applications that have keywords associated with the requirements of the position.

The good news about this technology is that it enables you to market your resume to thousands of employers quite easily. The bad news is that you must create an **electronic resume** in order to take advantage of the technology. But don't panic! An electronic resume is simply a modified version of your conventional resume.

And though an electronic resume is very different from other types of resumes, it's easy to create.

Content

The information you include in your electronic resume does not really differ from a traditional resume, it's simply the manner in which you present this information that changes. Traditional books on resume writing tell you to include lots of action verbs, such as managed, coordinated, or developed, but now, employers are more likely to do keyword searches filled with nouns, such as degree held or software you're familiar with. Personal traits are rarely used in keyword searches by employers, but when they are, traits like team player, creative, and problem-solving are among the most common. Following is a list of the basic information you should include in your resume:

- **Name.** Your name should appear at the top of your resume, with your address immediately underneath.
- **Abbreviations.** Most resume scanning systems will recognize a few common abbreviations like BS, MBA, and state names. Widely used acronyms for industry jargon, such as A/R and A/P on an accounting resume, are also generally accepted. But if there's any question about whether an abbreviation is a standard one, play it safe and spell it out.
- **Keywords.** Using the right keywords or key phrases in your resume is critical to its ultimate success—or lack thereof. Keywords are usually nouns or short phrases that the computer searches for when scanning your resume. Keywords usually refer to experience, training, skills, and abilities. For example, let's say an employer searches an employment database for a sales representative with the following keyword criteria:

sales representative
BS/BA
exceeded quota
cold calls
high energy
willing to travel

Even if you have the right qualifications, if you don't use these keywords on your resume, the computer will pass over your application. To complicate matters further, different employers search for different keywords. These are usually buzzwords common to your field or industry that describe your experience, education, skills, and abilities. Although there is no way to know for sure which keywords employers are most likely to search for, you can make educated guesses. Check help-wanted advertisements for job openings in your field. What terms do employers commonly use to describe their requirements? Executive recruiters who specialize in your field are also a good source of this kind of information. Of course, you'll want to use as many keywords in your resume as possible to maximize your chances. Keep in mind, however, that using the same keyword five times won't increase your chances of getting matched with an employer.

- **Keyword Summary.** This is a compendium of your qualifications, usually written in a series of succinct keyword phrases that immediately follows your name and address.

- **Career Objective.** As with traditional resumes, including a career objective is optional. If you choose to use a job objective, try to keep it general so as not to limit your opportunities. After all, while the computer does the initial screening, your resume will eventually be seen by a human hiring manager. Your objective should express a general interest in a particular field or industry ("an entry-level position in advertising"), but should not designate a specific job title ("a position as Senior Agency Recruitment Specialist"). You should try to include a few keywords in the objective as well, in order to increase your chances of getting matched ("a position as a financial analyst where I can utilize my on-the-job experience and MBA").

- **Experience and Achievements.** Your professional experience should immediately follow the keyword summary, beginning with your most recent position. (If you are a recent college graduate, however, you should list your education before your experience.) Be sure that your job title, employer, location, and dates of employment are all clearly displayed. Highlight your accomplishments and key responsibilities with bullets. Again, try to incorporate as many buzzwords as possible into these phrases.

- **Education.** This section immediately follows the experience section. List your degrees, licenses, permits, certifications, relevant course work, and academic awards or honors. Be sure to clearly display the names of the schools, locations, and years of graduation. You should also list any professional organizations or associations that you belong to; many recruiters will include such organizations when doing a keyword search.

- **References.** Don't waste valuable space with statements like "References available upon request." Although this section was standard fare for resumes of old, it won't win you any points on an electronic resume. Similarly, don't include personal data, such as your birthdate or marital status, or information regarding your hobbies and interests. Since it is unlikely that these sections would include any keywords, they are only taking up space, and the computer will pass right over them.

Format

Keep your resume simple. Remember, a computer will often look at your resume before a person does. The same elaborate formatting that makes your resume beautiful for the human eye to behold makes it impossible for a computer to understand. Following are some basic rules concerning how to format your resume:

- **Length of the Resume.** Ideally your resume should be one to two pages in length. If you go over one page, make sure your name appears at the top of each subsequent page. Always use a second sheet of paper if your resume is longer than one page—never try to print the second page on the back of the first.

- **Paper.** Don't bother with expensive paper or fancy colors. Use standard, twenty pound, 8½" x 11" paper. Because your resume needs to be as sharp and legible as possible, your best bet is to use black ink on white paper.

- **Font.** Stick to the basics; this is no time to express your creativity. Choose a nondecorative font with clear, distinct characters, such as Helvetica or Times. It is more difficult for a scanner to accurately pick up more decorative fonts. Usually the results are letters and words that all bleed into each other.

- **Font Size.** A font size of 12 points is ideal. Don't go below 10 or above 14 points, as type that is too small or too large is difficult for a scanner to read.

- **Font Style.** Most scanners will accept boldface, but if a potential employer specifically tells you to avoid it, you can substitute boldface with all capital letters. Boldface and all capitals are best used only for major section headings, such as "Experience" and "Education." It's also best to avoid using italics or underlining, since this can cause the letters to bleed into each other, or worse, make the words unintelligible. Once again, a plain style is best.

- **Graphics, Lines, and Shading.** Avoid the temptation to use lines and graphics to liven up what is an otherwise visually uninteresting resume. A resume scanner will try to "read" graphics, lines, and shading as text, resulting in computer chaos. You should also avoid using nontraditional layouts for your resume, such as two-column formats.

- **White Space.** Don't try to compress space between letters, words, or lines in order to fit everything on one page. When you do this, there's more of a chance that the words and letters will all bleed into each other, thus making it more difficult for the computer to read your resume. Many job seekers feel compelled to squeeze as much information as possible onto a single sheet of paper, but you should always leave plenty of space between sections on your resumes. It's easier for a scanner to "read" your resume with accuracy if there are distinct breaks between sections.

- **Printing.** Whatever type of printing process you use, make sure the end result is letter quality. Ideally, you should have it printed at your local copy shop. Otherwise, a laser printer is perfectly acceptable. Avoid typewriters and dot matrix printers, since the quality of type they produce is inadequate for most scanners. Because your resume needs to be as sharp and legible as possible, you should always send originals, not photocopies. For the same reason, you should always mail, not fax, your resume. And if your resume is longer than one page, don't staple the pages together.

Should You Include a Cover Letter with Your Electronic Resume?

Yes. Although a cover letter is generally not scanned, some systems will take a "photograph" of it, and store it electronically with your resume. And while your cover letter will not help you in the initial selection process, it can help distinguish you from the competition in the final rounds of elimination. If you've taken the time to craft a letter that summarizes your strongest qualifications, you'll have the edge over other contenders who skip this important step.

As with your resume, your cover letter should contain keywords reflecting your strongest qualifications. If you're responding to a classified ad, try to use many of the same keywords that the ad mentions. And if you're sending your resume to a new networking contact, be sure to mention who referred you. Even in this anonymous electronic age, the old adage "it's all in who you know" still holds true.

ELECTRONIC COVER LETTER

47 Lake Shore Drive
Cambridge, MA 02138
(617) 555-5555

September 3, 1997

Ms. Pat Cummings
Controller
Any Corporation
1140 Main Street
Boston, MA 02215

Dear Ms. Cummings:

This letter is in response to your September 2 advertisement in the *Boston Globe* for the position of Assistant Controller. I am very interested in the position and believe I have the qualifications you are looking for. Please consider the following:

- Over twenty years experience in Accounting and Systems Management, Budgeting, Forecasting, Cost Containment, Financial Reporting, and International Accounting.
- Implemented "team-oriented" cross-training program within accounting group, resulting in timely month-end closings and increased productivity of key accounting staff.
- MBA in Management from Northeastern University.
- Results-oriented professional and proven team leader.

These are only a few of my credentials that may be of interest to you. I look forward to discussing them with you further in a personal interview. Thank you for your consideration.

Sincerely,

Chris Smith

Enc. resume

ELECTRONIC RESUME

CHRIS SMITH
47 Lake Shore Drive
Cambridge, MA 02138
(617) 555-5555

KEYWORD SUMMARY

Senior financial manager with over twenty years experience in Accounting and Systems Management, Budgeting, Forecasting, Cost Containment, Financial Reporting, and International Accounting. MBA in Management. Proficient in Lotus, Excel, Solomon, Real World, and Windows.

EXPERIENCE

COLWELL CORPORATION, Wellesley, MA
$100 Million Division of Bancroft Corporation

Director of Accounting and Budgets, 1988 to present
Directed staff of twenty in General Ledger, Accounts Payable, Accounts Receivable, and International Accounting. Facilitated month-end closing process with parent company and auditors.

- Implemented "team-oriented" cross-training program within accounting group, resulting in timely month-end closings and increased productivity of key accounting staff.
- Developed and implemented a strategy for Sales and Use Tax Compliance in all fifty states with 100 percent compliance for both parent company and subsidiaries.
- Prepared monthly financial statements and analyses for review by management executive board.

Accounting Manager, 1985–1988
Managed a staff of six in General Ledger and Accounts Payable. Responsible for the design and refinement of financial reporting package. Assisted in month-end closing.

- Established guidelines for month-end closing procedures, thereby speeding up closing by five business days.
- Promoted to Director of Accounting and Budgets.

CHRIS SMITH
(page 2)

FRANKLIN AND DELANY COMPANY, Melrose, MA

Senior Accountant, 1979–1985
Managed A/P, G/L, transaction processing, and financial reporting. Supervised staff of two.
- Developed Management Reporting package, including variance reports and cash flow reporting.

Staff Accountant, 1975–1979
Managed A/P, including vouchering, cash disbursements, and bank reconciliation. Wrote and issued policies. Maintained supporting schedules used during year-end audits. Trained new employees.

Junior Accountant, 1973–1975
Assisted in general ledger closing. Monitored cash collections and accounts receivable.

EDUCATION

MBA in Management, Northeastern University, Boston, MA, 1985
BS in Accounting, Boston College, Boston, MA, 1973

ASSOCIATIONS

National Association of Accountants

Circulating Your Electronic Resume

Once you have designed a computer-friendly resume, there are three possible ways to circulate it. The first involves an **electronic employment database** service. For what is usually a minimal fee, you can send your electronic gem to one of these services, where it will be filed in a database containing up to tens of thousands of resumes. When outside companies need candidates for a job opening, they contact the service, and provide a list of qualifications (or keywords) the position requires. The service will then search the database (using a keyword search) to find suitable candidates.

The second way to circulate your resume is to send it to a company with an **in-house resume database**. With these systems, your resume is scanned into the company's database. Whenever there's an opening, the hiring manager submits a search request, which generally includes a job description and a list of keywords to search for. Again, operators will search the database to come up with viable candidates.

The last way to make use of your electronic resume is to **post it directly onto the Internet**, either to an online database service, a commercial online service, a newsgroup, or a site on the World Wide Web. Basically, online databases work the same way as electronic employment databases. Once you post your resume to a specified site on the Internet, it becomes available to the increasing number of corporate recruiters who regularly search the Internet for job candidates.

This chapter will discuss the first two methods of circulation: resume database services and applicant tracking systems. *For more information on how and where to post your resume online, please refer to Chapter 2.*

Electronic Employment Databases

How would you feel if you were told you could contact dozens, or even hundreds, of potential employers with a single copy of your resume—ecstatic, relieved, hopeful? Well, with the help of an electronic employment database, that is exactly what you can do.

An electronic employment database is simply a resume database operated by independent commercial firms. These databases can contain tens of thousands of resumes from all levels of job seekers—college graduates to experienced corporate executives. The procedure for submitting resumes to these services varies, and most do charge a nominal fee. But what you get for your money is fabulous: nationwide exposure to hundreds of companies of all sizes, from *Fortune* 500 to smaller, rapidly expanding companies.

In many ways, an electronic resume database is very similar to a traditional employment agency: You send in your resume to a service, and the service begins working to find a job for you. However, with an electronic employment "agency," you are—theoretically—in the running for every job request that comes into a company, thanks to the use of keyword searches. While each resume database service is different, it generally works as follows:

- **You submit your resume to an electronic employment database service.** Most companies charge a small fee, usually around $30 to $50. Some services will also send you a "professional profile" sheet to fill out. Essentially an employment application, these forms ask you to indicate your work experiences, skills, and other information, such as geographical preferences or if you are willing to relocate. This form is used either in addition to or instead of your resume.
- **Your resume and/or professional profile is scanned** or entered into the computer system.
- **Client companies call the service with job openings**, and give the database service a list of keywords and desired qualifications. Some services allow employ-

ers online access to the database so they can do the search themselves.

- **The database is searched for suitable candidates** who match the keywords provided by the client.
- **The service provides the client with a list of possible candidates.** Again, how the candidates are presented varies according to the service. Some services provide candidate summaries, others provide the actual resume, while still others also include the additional information that the candidate provided on his or her "professional profile."
- **The client company sorts through the list of possible candidates, and then contacts desirable candidates directly.** Some services, however, will call you before forwarding your resume or any information to the client company.

Electronic employment databases offer tremendous advantages to both the job seeker and the recruiting company. A job seeker can easily be exposed to hundreds of companies with only one resume and minimal cost. In the past, it would take job hunters hours of research to come up with the company names, addresses, and contact names of potential employers. Plus, job hunters had the additional cost of stationery, printing, and postage to mail out those hundreds of resumes. Also, job hunters are exposed to employers nationwide, not just in their own town or region. So if you are willing to relocate, you can find your dream job even if it's thousands of miles away!

For employers, resume database services can potentially save companies hours of work. Instead of putting a costly advertisement in the newspaper or a trade publication whenever there's a job opening, and then spending time looking through the responses, which can often number in the hundreds, companies can simply call up a resume database service, and the service will do the work for them. In effect, these services prescreen candidates. The use of the keyword search ensures that employers won't waste time reviewing resumes of candidates who lack the proper qualifications for a position. And again, employers have easy exposure to thousands of candidates. While no company relies entirely on this method, many companies use it as a first step in the search for qualified candidates, often because the database will give them a better idea of the available talent pool. For instance, if a database search turned up only a few qualified candidates, the recruiter may re-evaluate the minimum qualifications and skills for a given position.

Many job seekers are wary of resume database services because of issues of confidentiality. What if you submit your resume to a database service, only to have it land on your boss' desk? Many services offer safeguards to ensure this doesn't happen. Some database services allow you to submit names of companies you would prefer did not receive your resume. Others will contact you to get your permission before forwarding your resume or employment profile to a company. Still others allow you to join the database anonymously—that is, your name, company names, education, and any other identifiable characteristics will not be shown to prospective employers. Again, check with your service to determine its particular policy.

Of course, each electronic employment database is different. For instance, some services only accept resumes from alumni of particular universities, while others market to a specific demographic. Also, the fees services charge can vary; the database run by Electronic Job Matching, for example, is free to job seekers. When researching potential resume database services, you should also find out if the employer will see your actual resume or just a candidate profile or summary.

The following is a directory of selected electronic employment databases. One word of caution: Be sure to check with each service before sending your resume or any registration fees. With today's ever-changing technology, procedures or fees can change quickly. You should also call a prospective service to obtain more detailed information on how the service works.

cors
One Pierce Place, Suite 300 East, Itasca IL 60143
800-323-1352/708-250-8677
Fax: 708-250-7362
This service boasts of having almost 1.5 million resumes in their database. With over 6,000 clients, the service matches about 200 jobs each month. The firm attracts clients in all fields—computers, health care, finance, engineering, and communications. You can join this service for a one-time fee of $25; simply mail your resume to the address indicated. Once the service receives your resume, you will receive a confirmation letter in the mail that includes an identification number, which you can use to check on the status of your resume or to make free updates to it.

DORS
DMDC/Operation Transition
P. O. Box 130, Seaside CA 93955
800-727-3677
Fax: 408-583-2475
This is a resume database service for military personnel and workers in select civil service organizations who are leaving the military or civil service to work in the private sector. The goal of the service is to help military personnel make a successful transition to civilian life by giving candidates exposure to a wide range of companies in diverse fields and locations. Military personnel receive information on this service as part of their transition training. This service is also available for the spouses of military personnel. There are no fees for job seekers; employers assume all fees. According to information supplied by DORS, more than 16,000 employers have registered to use the service.

Electronic Job Matching

HRMC (Human Resource Management Center)
1915 North Dale Mabry Highway, Suite 307, Tampa FL 33607
813-879-4100
Fax: 813-870-1883
The Electronic Job Matching Database is free to all job seekers. The database currently contains over 30,000 resumes. More than 700 employers actively search the database, including private-sector companies in all fields and industries, from communications and law to manufacturing and health care. To enter the database, simply mail your resume to the address indicated. Your resume will be scanned into the system, and the computer will create a personalized "electronic portfolio" based on your resume. According to a spokesperson, the company accepts resumes with just about any kind of formatting, including bold and italicized words.

HispanData

360 South Hope Avenue, Suite 300-C, Santa Barbara CA 93105
805-682-5843
Fax: 805-687-4546
HispanData is a resume database for Hispanic professional job seekers. For a $25 processing fee, you can become part of a pool of 15,000 highly qualified candidates for positions in business, computers, engineering, and finance. Mail your resume to the address indicated, and your resume will remain in the database indefinitely. You can also make regular updates to your resume for an additional $10 fee.

National Resume Bank

3637 Fourth Street North, Suite 330, St. Petersburg FL 33704
813-896-3694
Fax: 813-894-1277
Sponsored by the Professional Association of Resume Writers, the database consists of nearly 3,500 potential candidates. To enroll in

this service, send $40 and five copies of your resume to the address indicated. You will also be asked to fill out a listing sheet, where you check off information such as whether you are willing to relocate, and to what areas. You must also classify yourself in one of thirty job categories. (To classify yourself in more than one category costs an additional $10 per category.) Possible categories include professions ranging from clerical to engineering. You can also classify yourself geographically, either by state or by city. The National Resume Bank is an online database service, meaning that the hundreds of employers who use the service can search the database directly from their computers. During the search, employers can preview candidate summaries, and are sent the actual resumes and cover letters upon request.

Resumes-on-Computer
Curtis Development Company
1000 Waterway Boulevard, Indianapolis IN 46202
317-636-1000
Fax: 1-900-RESUME-1
With more than 5,000 resumes in its database, Resumes-on-Computer is unique among resume database services. To submit your resume, you simply fax it to the number 1-900-RESUME-1. The fax will cost you a flat $5 for your resume, regardless of how many pages it is. If you want to include additional information, such as whether you are willing to relocate and where you are willing to relocate to, you can simply include that information in a separate cover letter. And when you want to update your resume, simply fax the revised copy, for another charge of only $5. The fax is hooked up to a computer, and your resume is scanned directly to the database. Resumes-on-Computer's clients include hundreds of companies that recruit for a wide range of fields.

SkillSearch
3354 Perimeter Hill Drive, Suite 235, Nashville TN 37211-4129

800-252-5665

Fax: 615-834-0376

This extensive resume database contains more than 60,000 resumes. SkillSearch accepts resumes for all fields, except for academic and medical professions. Most members have at least two years' experience, although the average member has eight years' work experience. To enter the database, you must fill out a lengthy "Member Profile" questionnaire, on which you list your career history, salary requirements, professional achievements, and geographic preferences. You must also code yourself by occupation, industry, and education level. SkillSearch will create a professional resume based on the information you send in. SkillSearch reports conducting 50–70 searches each week. You can update or change your resume at any time at no cost. Membership costs $89 per year, although a discounted price of $65 is available for many, including the members of over 100 university alumni and professional associations.

University ProNet

3803 East Bayshore Road, Box 51820, Palo Alto CA 94303

415-845-4000

Fax: 415-691-1619

University ProNet is a database of more than 50,000 resumes, sponsored by sixteen of the country's leading universities: California Institute of Technology; Carnegie-Mellon University; Columbia University; Cornell University; Massachusetts Institute of Technology; Ohio State University; Stanford University; University of California at Berkeley; UCLA; University of Chicago; University of Illinois; University of Michigan; University of Pennsylvania; University of Texas at Austin; University of Wisconsin; and Yale University. The service is open only to the alumni of these universities, but it is accessible to over 250 companies. One-time fees run about $50; the fee varies slightly depending on the school. If you hold a degree from one of these universities, contact your alumni association for more information on how to join this service.

Applicant Tracking Systems

As the name implies, applicant tracking systems, or in-house resume databases, are used by companies to keep track of the hordes of resumes they receive. Many companies, especially large, well-known companies, can receive an average of two hundred resumes per week. Where once these unsolicited resumes may have headed straight for a filing cabinet, or even the trash—never to be looked at again—electronic applicant tracking systems now allow employers to keep resumes in an active file, in some cases indefinitely.

An in-house resume database functions much the same way as a commercial employment database. Basically, here's how it works:

- **A company receives your resume**, either unsolicited, through a career fair, or in response to a classified advertisement.
- **Your resume is scanned into the computer**, where it becomes part of a large pool of talent, often consisting of thousands of resumes.
- **Your resume is dated, coded, and placed into the appropriate file**, such as administrative, financial, or technical. Other systems may simply sort resumes according to date received.
- **Whenever there's a job opening, hiring managers simply submit search requests to the database operator**, who is usually someone in either human resources or information systems.
- **The database operator performs keyword searches** in order to find resumes that match the criteria that the hiring manager has provided.

- **The database operator provides the hiring manager with the resumes** (or candidate summaries) of those candidates who meet the criteria, at which point the hiring process continues in the traditional manner.

Companies prefer this new technology because it's more efficient, in terms of both time and money. The automated system cuts down on paperwork for many human resources managers, and subsequently lowers administrative costs. Also, in major cities like New York or Los Angeles, the cost of classified advertising can run into the thousands of dollars. With applicant tracking systems, companies can simply dip into their established pool of candidates before spending money on costly advertising or employment firms.

But these applicant tracking systems benefit you, the job seeker, the most. First, a computer is completely impartial. You don't have to worry about the computer getting tired, bored, or cranky by the time it gets around to "reading" your resume. Also, a computer can't tell if you are a man or a woman, which is especially important if you are a woman applying for a traditionally masculine position, or vice versa. Similarly, a computer won't immediately look at your work experience and decide you're too old or too young for a position.

There's also less of a chance that your resume will get lost on someone's desk or in a filing cabinet. When resumes are received, they're immediately scanned and put on file electronically. Providing, of course, that your resume was computer-friendly and scannable, you don't have to worry about your resume getting misplaced accidentally.

Finally, an applicant tracking system will increase the chances of your finding a position within a specific company. Consider this scenario: You send in your resume in response to a help-wanted advertisement. Your resume is filed into the company's in-house resume database. You're passed over for that position, but three months later, a similar position opens up. When the database is searched, your resume comes up as a possible match. Your resume is passed along to the hiring manager, who decides to bring you in for an interview, and four weeks later, you're offered the position.

In the days before this technology, you had little chance of landing another job within a company if you were passed over initially. Most likely, your resume would have been thrown out after you were passed over the first time, and you would never even have had an opportunity to apply for the second position. **However, with an electronic tracking system, your resume is automatically kept in the database, where—because of the use of keyword searches—you remain in contention for every job opening.**

An electronic applicant tracking system also eliminates the need to send in multiple resumes to the same company. Before, a job seeker may have sent in resumes to three or four different department managers. Now, just one submission is necessary, since your resume is kept in a company-wide database where it is accessible to every hiring manager. If, however, you do send in multiple resumes, the system will usually throw out the old one and keep the most recent one on file.

Still, there are two major disadvantages to automated applicant tracking systems. The first is the impersonal nature of the system. A computer will look for only those resumes that exactly meet the strict criteria of the search. This tends to put recent college graduates or those switching careers at a disadvantage, since these job seekers are less likely to have as many keywords included in their resumes. Whereas a recruiter would see that a candidate had just graduated, and may still bring that person in for an interview even if the resume didn't meet the established criteria exactly, a computer would pass over that same candidate. Similarly, the new technology also hurts borderline candidates, who may be passed over by a computer search because they only have six out of ten desired keywords. Again, these same candidates may have been brought in for interviews if the recruiter noticed some special accomplishment or trait which the computer wasn't asked to look for.

Another problem, of course, is the technology itself. No automated system is infallible—there's always a chance that the computer will reject your resume, thereby taking you out of contention for any job openings. If, for some reason, the scanner is unable to read your resume, or turns it into an unintelligible mess, you are out of luck. Don't expect the database operator to call you and ask you to send in a new resume if the computer ruined or couldn't understand the first one. Therefore, it is essential that you follow the steps discussed earlier in order to design a clean, computer-friendly resume.

CHAPTER TWO

POSTING YOUR
RESUME ONLINE

By now you realize that having an electronic resume, one that a computer can easily read and understand, is essential if you want to keep up in today's job market. But to remain truly competitive, you need to take your resume and your job search a step further. In other words, your resume also needs to be in a format that you can send to employers and online databases electronically through cyberspace. Why is this important? Companies are increasingly requesting that resumes be submitted through email, and many recruiters regularly check online resume databases for candidates to fill unadvertised job openings.

There are three basic ways to get your resume on the Internet. If you have a plain text resume, you can **post your resume to an online resume database** or **email it directly to a potential employer**. Or, you can **create a resume in HTML and post it to special sites on the Web** that accept HTML resumes. You can even design your own home page for potential employers to visit. HTML (hypertext markup language) is the text formatting language used to publish information on the World Wide Web.

Online resume databases are very similar to the electronic employment databases discussed in the previous chapter. Simply put, they are large databases of resumes that employers search when looking for job candidates. Submitting your resume to an online resume database is a relatively inexpensive method of exposing your resume to a large audience, including thousands of human resources professionals at major corporations and independent recruiters. Online resume databases are generally found on Usenet newsgroups or the World Wide Web, although one major database service, the Worldwide Resume/Talent Bank, is accessible through both America Online and the Internet.

Emailing your resume directly to potential employers is generally done in response to a help-wanted advertisement or simply as a method of direct contact. In fact, many companies now request that resumes be submitted through email, rather than the U.S. mail or fax machine. Many job listings you find on the Internet, particularly for technical positions, include only an email address for contact information; no street address or telephone number is provided. And with many companies, you can email your resume directly into their in-house resume database. This eliminates the concern that your resume will be found unreadable by a computerized resume scanner.

The real usefulness of HTML resumes is still being explored. Most of the major online databases, with the exception of some such as the Online Career Center's database, do not accept HTML resumes, and the vast majority of companies only accept plain text resumes through their email. At the same time, new sites that do accept HTML resumes are constantly cropping up on the Web, as are job seekers showing off their skills on their own home pages. Since at the time of this writing, job hunting experts are divided on the value of having your own Web page and HTML resume, the bulk of this chapter will discuss plain text resumes, online databases, and the protocol of emailing resumes to potential employers, while HTML resumes and creating your own home page will only be discussed briefly.

But before you go ahead and throw out your old paper resume, be advised that not all companies stay up to speed on the latest technology. Many companies simply don't have the equipment to directly receive emailed resumes and search online databases for job candidates. Thus, having a paper copy of your resume is still a necessity, especially since you'll need it to bring with you to all those job interviews!

Converting Your Resume to a Plain Text File

Remember, an electronic resume is one that is sparsely formatted, but filled with keywords and important facts. If you have already prepared a resume that is computer-friendly, you don't have that far to go to be able to post your resume on the Internet. A plain text resume is the next step in creating a truly electronic resume. But before you panic and start thinking that you need to create yet another resume, rest assured that you can easily convert your regular resume to one that can be transmitted electronically.

In order to post your resume to the Internet, you will need to change the way your resume is formatted. Instead of a Microsoft Word, WordPerfect, or other word processing document, **save your resume as a plain text, DOS, or ASCII file**. These three terms are basically interchangeable; different software will use different terms. These words all describe text at its simplest, most basic level, without the formatting like boldface and italics that we all like to use so that our documents look more interesting. If you have email, you'll notice that all your messages are written and received in this format. ASCII, which stands for American Standard Code for Information Interchange, is simply a code that virtually all computers can understand. It was invented to allow different types of computers to easily exchange information. By converting your resume to a plain text, or ASCII, file you can be assured your resume and other files will be readable regardless of where you send them. If you don't convert your resume to text-only, your resume and other files will end up looking like junk.

Before you attempt to create your own plain text resume, study the resumes on the online databases. This will give you a good idea of what a plain text resume looks like, and will help you to create your own resume. Following are the basic steps for creating a plain text resume. The particulars of the process will differ, depending on what type of computer system and software you're using:

- **Remove all formatting from your resume**. This includes all boldface, italics, underlining, bullets, different font sizes, lines, and any and all graphics. To highlight certain parts of your resume, such as education or experience, you may choose to use capital letters. You can also use dashes (—) or asterisks (*) if you want to emphasize certain accomplishments or experiences. Finally, be sure to leave a blank line or two between sections in order to separate them.

- **Convert your resume to a plain text file**. Most word processing programs, such as WordPerfect and Microsoft Word, have a "save as" feature that allows you to save files to different formats. For instance, in Microsoft Word for Windows, saving a document as a Word document, as a text-only document, or as a WordPerfect document are just some of your options. Many programs—like Microsoft Word—don't specifically give you an "ASCII" option; in these programs, you should choose "text only" or "plain text." In Microsoft Word, plain text files have the extension *.txt.

- **After saving your resume as a plain text file, check the document with the text editor** that most computers have. In Windows 3.1, use the Notepad from the accessories group found in Program Manager.

- **Open the file to be sure that your margins look right and that you don't have extra spaces between lines or letters**. If parts of the text look garbled with a group of strange characters, it most likely means that you forgot to take out some formatting. A resume with a lot of formatting is likely to end up looking like hieroglyphics if it's read as a plain text file. If this happens, you need to go back to your original document and repeat the process. See the next page for an example of a plain text resume, viewed in Notepad.

- **Be sure that all your lines contain sixty-five characters or less**. This includes all spacing, letters, and punctuation. Often, you will need to go through your entire resume line-by-line, counting each space, letter, punctuation, asterisks, and so forth. You may need to manually insert hard returns where the lines are longer than sixty-five characters. This may seem trivial, but it is actually extremely important. While some computers may recognize as many as seventy-five characters, the majority cannot recognize more than sixty-five characters per line. So just to be on the safe side, don't go longer than sixty-five characters.

- Finally, **email your resume to yourself or to a friend in order to test the file**. Be sure that your resume stayed intact, that no extra spaces or returns were inserted during the transmission, and that all text appears readable. If something doesn't look right, go back to your text editor, fix the problem, and test the resume again before emailing it to any companies or posting it to online databases.

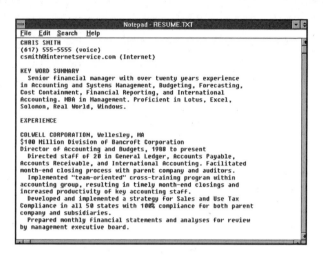

Notepad - RESUME.TXT

File Edit Search Help

CHRIS SMITH
(617) 555-5555 (voice)
csmith@internetservice.com (Internet)

KEY WORD SUMMARY
    Senior financial manager with over twenty years experience
in Accounting and Systems Management, Budgeting, Forecasting,
Cost Containment, Financial Reporting, and International
Accounting. MBA in Management. Proficient in Lotus, Excel,
Solomon, Real World, Windows.

EXPERIENCE

COLWELL CORPORATION, Wellesley, MA
$100 Million Division of Bancroft Corporation
Director of Accounting and Budgets, 1988 to present
    Directed staff of 20 in General Ledger, Accounts Payable,
Accounts Receivable, and International Accounting. Facilitated
month-end closing process with parent company and auditors.
    Implemented "team-oriented" cross-training program within
accounting group, resulting in timely month-end closings and
increased productivity of key accounting staff.
    Developed and implemented a strategy for Sales and Use Tax
Compliance in all 50 states with 100% compliance for both parent
company and subsidiaries.
    Prepared monthly financial statements and analyses for review
by management executive board.

Why Use Online Resume Databases?

Why post your resume to an online database? In a word: exposure! Recent reports indicate that over twenty million people worldwide have access to the Internet, including thousands of human resources professionals and recruiters. Why *wouldn't* you want your skills to have that breadth of exposure?

By posting your resume online, you are essentially marketing yourself to the thousands of human resources professionals and hiring managers worldwide who are using the Internet in ever increasing numbers, either to post job listings or to search resume databases for job candidates. **Online databases allow recruiters and hiring managers to search through large pools of candidates quickly and easily**, using keywords to identify only those candidates who have the right qualifications for a given position. What's more, many recruiters report that job candidates found online tend to be of a higher quality than those found through, say, a newspaper advertisement. Candidates who use the Internet have the advanced computer skills that are becoming increasingly important in today's job market. Many recruiters like to see candidates who take the initiative to embrace this new technology.

Another reason to use an online resume database is its reach. If you are considering relocating, posting your resume in an online database is a good way to get it circulating in another city before you even move. Most job hunting sites on the World Wide Web are searched by recruiters nationwide—even worldwide—and there are also a number of regional databases (mostly newsgroups) where you can post your resume. So if you live in Baltimore and you want to find a job in San Francisco, you could post your resume to **ba.jobs.resumes**, a Usenet newsgroup for resume posting in the San Francisco Bay area.

At the same time, many job hunters are wary of putting their lives on display for anyone to see. When your resume is online, it's accessible to virtually anyone with a computer and an Internet connection. This includes personal information, such as your name, address, and telephone number. It is this lack of control over who sees their resume that worries most job seekers. Since you have no control over who sees your resume, you may receive phone calls or email messages from companies, organizations, and individuals you have absolutely no interest in working for.

However, the biggest concern to most job hunters is: What if one of those twenty million people cruising the Internet happens to be your boss? Although some databases, such as the Monster Board's resume posting site, hide your personal information from employers until after they've bought your resume, the majority of resume databases do not offer anonymity to their users. And while some services (like the Online Career Center) restrict access to their resume database only to subscribers, that is only seldom the case.

For the most part, posting your resume online is a fairly risk-free proposition, and the odds are generally low that your boss will stumble upon your resume while trying to find the scores from the previous day's football games. At the same time, if you know for a fact that your boss regularly searches the Internet whenever new positions open up, posting your resume online is probably not a good idea. However, these are the chances you take when you launch your resume into cyberspace.

Where to Post Your Resume Online

Now that you know the reasons for posting your resume to an online database, you are probably wondering *where* to post it. Cyberspace offers three main areas for resume posting: commercial online services, Usenet newsgroups, and the World Wide Web. These sites range from the general (**misc.jobs.misc**) to the specific (**http://www.medsearch.com**). Of the three areas, you'll find the most options on the World Wide Web. Virtually all of the major job hunting sites on the Web, such as the Monster Board and E-Span, offer resume databases where job hunters can post their resumes. The Web also contains dozens of other sites for resume posting, including the only sites where you can post HTML resumes.

Bulletin Board Systems (BBSs), Gopher, and Telnet are not generally considered destinations for resume posting, and are best used to find job listings or to gather information regarding specific industries and potential employers. While you may post resumes to most Bulletin Board Systems, they are not a very efficient way to circulate your resume. For this reason, you're better off sticking to sites on the Web and Usenet newsgroups.

Most sites have their own specific instructions for entering a resume into their database. These instructions should tell you how long resumes remain in the database, how to update and remove your resume from the database, who has access to the database, and the fee amount (if any). If a database does not have specific instructions, email or call the site administrators for more information.

Some sites may require you to fill out personal information online, such as your name, email address, and resume title, but most allow you to attach your own resume, or paste it in a specfic area. Never try to create your entire resume online, since you would likely incur a mountain of online charges.

When emailing your resume to a database, don't overlook one very important part of your email: the subject line. The subject line generally becomes your resume title, therefore it's important that it gives an indication of your field and job title. Many people mistakenly type "resume" or even their name on the subject line. The subject line is typically the first information seen by employers scanning the database, and it is often the only information a recruiter will look at. For this reason, it's important to be fairly specific on your subject line. Mention your profession, experience and—since many resumes are seen by recruiters nationwide—your location. For instance, "Financial Analyst-3 Yrs. Exp.-CFA-IL." You could also mention if you are willing to relocate, "Financial Analyst-3 Yrs. Exp.-CFA-Will Relocate."

After emailing your resume to a database, try to download your resume. Once your resume is downloaded, make sure that all information is there and presented clearly. This serves a dual purpose. In addition to ensuring that your resume survived electronic transmission, you can conduct a keyword search and check that the resume turns up when appropriate. Naturally, be sure to check that downloading your resume is free before attempting this.

Given all the choices available, you may be wondering how to decide where to post your resume—newsgroups, commercial online services, or the World Wide Web. There's no rule that says you can post your resume in only one database. Since most online resume databases don't charge job seekers, you could—theoretically—post your resume to every site. However, since that's not necessarily practical, the best approach is to visit a database of potential interest to see what types of resumes are in the database.

For instance, if you visit a site where most resumes showcase technical backgrounds, then it's a safe bet that most of the companies that search that database are looking to fill technical positions. If you have a background in finance, you would not want to post your resume there. Similarly, if you notice that most resumes show little experience, you may have stumbled upon a posting site for new graduates. If you have ten solid years of work experience, it would likely do little good to post your resume there. Finally, if you are thinking of posting your resume to a general job posting site, such as the Online Career Center, check out what companies advertise in their job listings sections. Generally, those same sponsors will be the primary companies to scan the database for candidates.

Most online sites do not charge for posting your resume; charges, if any, are usually incurred by client employers and recruiters. However, some—especially those run by independent recruiters or career placement services—do charge a small fee. Sometimes those fees include resume preparation and advice. At the same time, those type of resume databases are smaller and do not have as wide an exposure as some of the larger, free databases. But if you feel you need help composing your resume, the fee might just be worth it.

One word of caution: Before you write a check or give your credit card number to a company over the Internet, it's a good idea to check its reputation with the Better Business Bureau or a similar agency. While the majority of companies selling services over the Internet are reputable, remember that simply because a company has a presence on the Internet does not mean it is honest and legitimate.

Commercial Online Services

Commercial online services, like America Online, CompuServe, The Microsoft Network, and Prodigy are, in comparison to newsgroups and the Web, fairly limited in what they offer in terms of resume posting services. However, these services have easy access to both newsgroups and the Web, so you can easily use the resume posting resources available there. One exception is the Worldwide Resume/Talent Bank Service on America Online. *For more in-depth information regarding the job-related resources these services offer, see Chapter 4, Commercial Online Services.*

America Online's Worldwide Resume/Talent Bank Service was created by James C. Gonyea, the director and creator of America Online's Career Center. The service is available through both America Online and the Internet, at the Internet Career Connection (**http://icweb.com**). Besides full- or part-time help, many members have found consulting and volunteer work, as well as positions on advisory boards. The service costs around $40 for a one-year subscription, and accepts only plain text resumes. For more information, including instructions on how to enter your resume into the database, use the keyword "careers" and then choose Career Center, and then Talent Bank.

Newsgroups

Usenet newsgroups tend to be more focused in scope, in terms of both region and subject matter. So by posting your resume in a newsgroup, it is more likely to be seen by a local employer, or one that really matches your interests, than if you put your resume in a large national database. What's the point of having twenty employers call to request interviews if they are all in San Diego and you live in Baltimore?

One word of caution: **Usenet newsgroups tend to follow strict protocol**. Most newsgroups contain postings with advice that outlines the protocol for that particular newsgroup. Be sure to read these *before* posting your resume. For instance, the posting "Resume Style Consensus" found in the newsgroup **misc.jobs.resumes** tells you that most resumes in the newsgroup fall into one of three categories: entry-level, contract, or permanent positions, and advises job hunters to include one of those three categories in their subject line. Finally, be careful not to post your resume to just any newsgroup with the word "job" in the address, since not every job-related newsgroup accepts resume postings. Following is a list of some newsgroups that accept resume postings:

alt.medical.sales.jobs.resumes
Medical sales positions, United States

atl.resumes
Atlanta, Georgia

ba.jobs.resumes
San Francisco Bay area, California

houston.jobs.wanted
Houston, Texas

il.jobs.resumes
Illinois

misc.jobs.resumes
United States

nm.jobs
New Mexico

nyc.jobs.wanted
New York City

pdaxs.jobs.resumes
Portland, Oregon

pgh.jobs.wanted
Pittsburgh, Pennsylvania

phl.jobs.wanted
Philadelphia, Pennsylvania

seattle.jobs.wanted
Seattle, Washington

us.jobs.resume
United States

Ten Major Sites on the World Wide Web

Following are just ten of the major job hunting sites on the Web. These listings only discuss their resume posting capabilities. *See Chapter 6 for more information regarding their numerous other features, and a more comprehensive list of sites.* Unlike Usenet newsgroup databases, resume posting sites on the World Wide Web typically contain resumes from job hunters across the country, which means that employers nationwide search the databases for potential candidates. For this reason, it's a good idea to add a line to your resume stating whether you are willing to relocate. And like newsgroups, you will need to come up with a title—or subject line—for your resume. Most experts suggest simply using your desired job title as the title for your resume.

CareerCity
http://www.careercity.com
"The Web's Big Career Site" gives job hunters access to 125,000 jobs via three job search engines: its own CareerCity jobs database; a newsgroup job search engine covering 100 newsgroups; and a company recruiting links search engine covering over 700 companies. CareerCity's easy-to-use resume database gives job hunters the opportunity to market their qualifications for free to employers subscribing to the database. And the site is rife with job-hunting advice from Adams Media Corporation's career books.

CareerMart
http://www.careermart.com

CareerMart's Resume Bank offers free resume postings to job hunters, and its E-mail Agent automatically notifies you when new positions crop up. Run by BSA Advertising, the site offers links to more than 400 major employers and some 700 colleges and universities. Resumes should be submitted as text files.

CareerMosaic
http://www.careermosaic.com

ResumeCM is CareerMosaic's database, which contains resumes from job hunters in all geographic areas and occupations. Besides the database on the Web, it also indexes the most popular Usenet newsgroups and automatically adds your resume to their databases. Unlike most databases, ResumeCM also allows employers to conduct a full-text search of your resume, instead of only searching subject lines.

Career Shop
http://www.careershop.com

This site, produced by TenKey Interactive, Inc., enables you to post your resume and also email it directly to employers, for free. Career Shop also offers a jobs database and allows employers who register with them to search the resume database for free.

CareerSite
http://www.careersite.com

A free service of Virtual Resources Corporation, CareerSite's resume database allows you to submit your resume as a fully formatted document. You simply need to fill in some fields online to summarize your credentials. Information is presented to participating employers blind—without your name and address. Plus, your resume is not released to a company without your consent, a great relief to those job seekers concerned with confidentiality.

E-Span Interactive Employment Network
http://www.espan.com
Available to employers nationwide, E-Span's Resume Pro Database accepts only plain text resumes. Your resume must be contained in the body of your email message; the service cannot process attachments.

IntelliMatch
http://www.intellimatch.com
A comprehensive site that allows you to not only post your resume as a text file to a vast database, but also to create a "PowerResume" by using the site's ResumeExpress format.

JobBank USA
http://www.jobbankusa.com
Like E-Span, JobBank USA's resume database provides widespread exposure to employers nationwide, and only accepts plain text resumes contained within the body of email. Again, do not send your resume as an attachment.

The Monster Board
http://www.monster.com
The Monster Board's Resume On-Line Database only accepts plain text resumes in the body of email messages; no attachments or HTML resumes are accepted. The Monster Board protects applicants by keeping their personal information, including name and address, separated from the body of the resume. Employers can only access that information after they have purchased the resume.

The Online Career Center
http://www.occ.com
The Online Career Center allows you to post both plain text (ASCII) and HTML resumes to their national database. The OCC even allows you to mail in a typed resume for inclusion in their

database, though there is a $15 processing fee for that service. Like many of these companies, the OCC limits access to its resume database to subscribers only.

Targeted Sites on the World Wide Web

Many sites on the Web where you can post your resume are regional or geared towards a specific field or experience level. Some accept only HTML resumes or ASCII resumes, while others accept both. Keep in mind that some of the lesser known sites described in the following list charge fees for entering your resume into the database.

This list is only a sample of additional sites you will find on the Web. **To find more databases, use a search engine such a Yahoo or Alta Vista, and enter the keywords "resumes" or "resume posting."** Not surprisingly, there are more of these sites popping up all the time, but the following list should get your search off to a decent start.

Again, the biggest advantage of these systems is that employers and recruiters like them because they are efficient. With these databases, employers have almost instant access to hundreds, if not thousands, of resumes. And this efficiency translates into lower administrative costs, which is the goal of all companies.

Canadian Resume Centre
http://netaccess.on.ca/~resume
Geared toward Canadians and those seeking opportunities to work in Canada, this site allows you to email your resume to their database, at a charge of $25 for six months. The company will accept faxed or mailed resumes, for a slightly higher fee.

Colorado Jobs Online
http://www.coloradojobs.com
This is a resume and job posting database for all types of positions in the state of Colorado. When the first edition of this book was

published, Colorado Jobs Online charged a $40 fee for posting a resume in its database for three months. At the time of this update, however, resume posting was free, for "a limited time."

Extreme Resume Drop
http://www.mainquad.com

A free service of The Main Quad, a career site for students and recent graduates, Extreme Resume Drop allows you to send your resume directly to over 200 recruiters at major corporations like Hewlett Packard, Deloitte & Touche, LLP, and Quantum. You can choose the companies you want to send your resume to from categories like the arts, business, and education. Simply paste your resume and cover letter in the spaces provided, click on a few buttons, and your resume will be automatically sent to the companies you selected.

4.0 Resumes and Job Listings
http://www.4pt0.com

This site is geared especially toward recent college graduates, one of many such sites that cater specifically toward that market. If that is your background, you can rest assured that your qualifications should be similar to those of other applicants registered here. Another site worth checking out is The Best Resumes on the Net (**http://www.tbrnet.com**), which features a resume bank that focuses on the graduating college student and career tips covering resumes, cover letters, and more.

The Internet Job Locator
http://www.joblocator.com/jobs/

This is a resume and job posting database for positions nationwide. A free service, the Internet Job Locator was created by Travelers OnLine and also accepts HTML resumes. It will also post your resume to selected Usenet newsgroups, allowing you to choose those newsgroups where your resume will be posted.

Job Center Employment Services
http://www.jobcenter.com

Job Center provides a resume posting service for candidates of all experience levels, and allows you to post a plain text or HTML resume. The service costs $20 for six months, which includes placement in the Job Center resume database and distribution to Usenet resume posting sites. The service also searches the job listings every day for ads that match your resume. Matching ads are automatically sent to you via email. Job Center also has a searchable database of job listings for job hunters.

MedSearch America
http://www.medsearch.com

This is a resume and job posting sevice for positions nationwide in the health care field. You can post your resume by completing an on-screen form and pasting your resume in a provided field, or you can simply email your resume. MedSearch America is produced by The Monster Board.

Shawn's Internet Resume Center
http://www.inpursuit.com/sirc/seeker.html

Also calling itself "The Executive's Resume Center," this is a resume posting site aimed specifically at executive-level job hunters, including presidents, vice presidents, and high level managers. A one-time fee is charged. The site also features a broad list of other employment related sites, complete with links.

The World Wide Web Resume Bank
http://www.careermag.com

Sponsored by Career Magazine, the World Wide Web Resume Bank is a fee-based service that broadcasts your resume to employers and recruiters worldwide. There is a sliding fee scale, starting at around $20, depending on whether you submit your resume online (the least expensive option), through email or diskette, or through traditional mail. It also has a confidential resume option that hides your contact information from employers, which costs an additional $12.

Emailing Your Resume Directly to a Company

Another way to get your resume noticed is to email it directly to an employer. As mentioned previously, more and more companies are requesting that resumes be submitted through email. This is especially true for companies that post their job listings on the Internet. In fact, many online job listings will not even contain an address or a phone number. And if you look at your Sunday help-wanted advertisements, you are likely to find that the ads will often give an email address, along with a mailing address or fax number, where candidates can submit resumes.

Email has several advantages over traditional "snail mail." **Emailing your resume is quick and efficient, for both you and your target company**. Instead of spending time printing out a copy of your resume, addressing an envelope, and mailing it, you can simply send your resume with a few clicks of your mouse. This allows you to respond almost instantly to job listings online, as well as ads you see in the newspaper. This means that you can be among the first candidates a hiring manager evaluates. By sending your resume through traditional means, you increase the chance that a hiring manager has already picked the candidates worthy of further consideration. And of course, employers like emailed resumes because they cut down on paperwork and lower administrative costs.

With that said, it's important to be aware of the proper procedure for emailing your resume to a specific company. While it's generally preferable to send a resume to a specific individual, rather than to a company's human resources department, you are more likely to find the email address for the human resources department than for a specific department manager or supervisor. The generic employment mailbox is usually the address given in help-wanted ads or on the company's home page, and unsolicited resumes sent to a general human resources mailbox are likely to end up in an in-house resume database. However, if the resume was emailed in response to a specific advertisement, the chances are greater that the resume will actually be viewed by an individual.

If you do find the email address of a specific manager or supervisor, don't simply send them your resume "cold." In this and other ways, emailing your resume is really no different than contacting companies the traditional way. Be sure to call or email that manager first to be sure that he or she is the right person to receive your resume, and to find out how you should send the resume—in the body of the email message or as an attachment.

Once you know the correct email address and other information, you can prepare your email message. Remember, you should only email your resume *after* you have first tested it by sending it to yourself or to a friend. Here are the steps to take to email your resume:

- First, **log on to your email account** and choose the option for a new message.
- **Type in the email address and subject**. For the subject, say something like, "Resume, entry-level accountant."
- **Paste your resume into the body of your email message**, or type in the resume file name as an attachment file.
- **Send** the email.

After you email your resume, wait a few days so you can be sure that someone has read it. Call or email the company to confirm that your resume was received intact. As with a paper resume, an emailed resume may do you little good unless you follow up to express your genuine interest in the company or the position. If you sent your resume to an individual, ask if he or she would like you to elaborate on any sections of your resume. Similarly, if you sent your resume to a general email address, call the human resources department to check the status of your application. Assuming they have an in-house resume database and applicant tracking system, they should be able to tell you whether or not the email was received.

As for cover letters, experts disagree on whether you should email one along with your resume. Some human resources professionals maintain that the cover letter, especially if it's contained in a separate file, is a nuisance. Others say a cover letter is still a job hunting necessity. Of course, if a company specifically requests one in a job listing, don't simply ignore the request. If, however, an ad makes no mention of a cover letter, your best bet is to call the human resources department and ask about sending one.

Creating an HTML Resume and Your Own Personal Home Page

One of the biggest trends right now in electronic job hunting is the use of HTML resumes, as well as individual home pages on the World Wide Web. Many job hunters are now creating resumes in hypertext markup language (HTML), the text formatting language for publishing documents on the Web. Many are also rushing to create their own home page, where potential employers can search for additional information on candidates. This is no doubt in response to the hype surrounding the Web, created in part by companies and organizations that heavily advertise their own home pages in commercial or print advertisements. Coupled with books such as this one, these advertising campaigns can leave job hunters with the impression that unless they have their own home page, their job hunt and career will be left in the dust. But before we delve into the usefulness of an HTML resume or home page, let's first discuss exactly what they are and how they are used.

An HTML resume is, quite simply, a resume written in the language of the World Wide Web. At a glance, it looks similar to a regular electronic resume. It lists the name of the job hunter, personal information, work history, and educational background. It can also contain a keyword summary, special skills, or any other information you would include in your traditional paper or electronic resume. More advanced HTML resumes can contain graphics, frames, or other special features. As mentioned earlier, you can post an HTML resume to a number of smaller databases, but of the major online resume databases, very few will will accept HTML resumes. Also, an HTML document cannot be emailed, so unless an employer has World Wide Web access, your resume or home page will not be seen by prospective employers.

Creating your own home page takes HTML resumes a step further. A typical job hunter's home page will include a resume, along with graphics, and perhaps some audio, video, and samples of your work, such as drawings or writing clips. You can also include links to a former employer's or alma mater's home page. However, when creating your own home page, you need to be sure that your employment background is emphasized over all else. It's easy to get carried away with creating a home page full of elaborate graphics or other links, but **your resume should still be the core of your home page**. You can alert employers to your home page by including your URL (Uniform Resource Locator) in your traditional paper or electronic resume.

Many nontechnical people may feel put off by all this talk of creating documents in a different language and creating a personal home page, but the truth is, it's not as difficult as it sounds. HTML is a relatively easy computer language to learn. You can find dozens of books in your local bookstore on the subject, and the Web contains a number of sites where you can learn the code.

Many Web browsers, including Netscape Navigator, have sites where you can learn HTML. From Netscape's home page (**http://home.netscape.com**) choose "Creating Net Sites" from the Assistance menu. Then, select "A Beginner's Guide to HTML," which will teach you the basics of the language, and then move on to "Composing Good HTML," a style guide on how to use the code properly. You can also take lessons on adding frames, graphics, sound, and so forth. Or, using a search engine like Yahoo!, try the keyword HTML to find other sites for learning the code. But if you feel you are simply not up to learning a new computer language, many of the resume posting sites discussed earlier will, for a fee, convert your resume to HTML.

Once you've mastered the basics of HTML, you can create your own home page. This is not as difficult as it sounds. Many Internet providers, such as The Internet Access Company (TIAC), or commercial online services like America Online, provide subscribers with the server hard disk space to create a personal home page. Check with your service for details on how to get your own space.

Now, you may be wondering if it's worthwhile for you to have your own home page or HTML resume. The answer, quite simply, is "it depends." First, remember that you can have an HTML resume without creating your own home page. And in many cases, a simple electronic resume is really all you need. Unless you're looking for a job as a Web page designer or another technical position, most companies simply don't care if their job applicants can create their own home page or know HTML. The bottom line? At the time of this writing, **having an HTML resume or your own home page simply is not as critical as having an electronic resume or a plain text resume for emailing.** However, if you have the time and inclination, learning the HTML language and creating your own home page can be a valuable technical skill to have for the future.

VIDEO AND MULTIMEDIA RESUMES

Whereas the previous two chapters have advised you to make your resume generic and "vanilla" so that a computer is able to read and understand it, this chapter takes a slightly different view: Instead of using a plain paper or electronic resume, create a lively multimedia or video resume that lets your true self shine through.

Before running out to find a friend with a video camera, a few words of caution. First, **video and multimedia resumes are, for the most part, fairly unusual in the world of human resources**, so don't even consider permanently scrapping your traditional resume in favor of a new, high-tech version. It's best to use these types of resumes as complements to your regular resume. At the same time, video and multimedia resumes can be—for certain people—a creative, yet professional way to express your qualifications and background to a potential employer. Now, this is not to say you should go out and produce an MTV-like music video detailing your work history, or create a multimedia presentation with senseless graphics or rock music sound bites. On the contrary, unless you're in a band that's trying to land a contract with a record company, no one will take you seriously.

While similar in nature, video and multimedia resumes are actually two different types of resumes. Like the name implies, a video resume is a videotape of a job applicant summarizing his or her work history and accomplishments. Most often, the video shows an applicant sitting in an office or other professional setting discussing his or her background and qualifications. Video resumes are generally in the form of dialogs or "question and answer" formats, in which an off-camera participant asks the candidate questions regarding his or her background. The video itself is short; usually no longer than five minutes, or the equivalent of a three-to-five page resume.

The multimedia resume can best be described as an electronic resume with a twist—it is bursting with advances in computer technology, using graphics, scanned photographs, and sound, as well as text, to convey an applicant's background to an employer. These resumes are usually sent to an employer on disk or posted online in an online resume database. Some job seekers maintain multimedia resumes as part of their home page on the World Wide Web. A typical multimedia resume (if there can be such a thing) includes virtually the same information contained in a regular resume, such as a summary of qualifications, accomplishments, work history, and educational background. However, instead of having this information plainly laid out on the computer screen, a multimedia resume is interactive. A multimedia resume might have a menu or different icons that the user clicks on in order to find various information. For instance, clicking on one icon might present a list of the applicant's qualifications through both text and sound. Many multimedia resumes also contain photographs, drawings, short videos, or other examples of an applicant's work.

Who Should Use Video and Multimedia Resumes?

Remember that while video or multimedia resumes are not suitable for everyone, they can be powerful job hunting tools if used judiciously. Most fields, even those like advertising or publishing that have reputations for being nontraditional, are still fairly conservative when it comes to the hiring process, and it is best to stick with traditional paper or electronic resumes. However, if you are in a creative, high-tech field where knowledge of cutting-edge technology is valued, a video or multimedia resume will be much more effective than a simple, one-dimensional piece of paper. **In fact, in some industries, a video or multimedia resume is essential in order to get noticed.**

In television broadcasting, for example, a form of the video resume is considered standard practice. Directors, producers, and reporters compile short videos that include information regarding their work and educational background, personal data (such as phone numbers and addresses where the candidate can be reached), as well as video clips of their best work. In fact, it's *expected* that candidates for these positions will send in video resumes, since that is the best way for the producer (or other hiring managers) to judge the quality of their work. But even if you are applying for a position where you will *not* be on the air (such as public relations), a video resume would still be appropriate, since you could be assured that whatever station you applied to has not only the equipment to easily view your video, but would appreciate it as well.

Similarly, a multimedia resume is practically a must if you are applying for positions in the field of multimedia technology, such as CD-ROM production or the Internet. In these fields, a multimedia resume is the easiest way to show off your skills to a potential employer. Not only will you be showing your talents to people who can appreciate it, but you can be confident that the company has the capacity to run your resume.

In a multimedia resume, artists or other craftsmen can include scanned photographs of their work alongside graphics and text. These "electronic portfolios" enable potential employers or clients to simply "point and click" to see examples of an artist's work. Multimedia and video resumes can also be appropriate in other creative and innovative fields, such as media or entertainment. The entertainment industry, for example, has been quick to embrace new technology, such as the Internet and the World Wide Web. Some industries, including entertainment, like to see candidates who exhibit imagination and a willingness to take chances. By using nontraditional resumes, you can set yourself apart from the crowd.

At the same time, if you work in a traditionally conservative field, such as banking, finance, or law, you should not even consider using anything other than a regular paper or electronic resume. In fields such as these, it is highly unlikely that a recruiter will even take the time to look at a video or multimedia resume, much less give serious consideration to the candidate who produced it.

The simplest advice to give someone considering using a video or multimedia resume is to know your audience. Only send your high-tech resume to companies on the leading edge, where your technological know-how and creativity is sure to be appreciated. Moreover, you also need to be sure that whatever company you're sending your resume to has the necessary equipment to view it. This is why it's best to call a company to find out if they will accept a nontraditional resume. That way, you won't waste your money sending a videotape or diskette to a company that will only toss it in the garbage. More importantly, you won't squander any valuable job leads. After all, it's hard enough to find a job without eliminating yourself from contention before you even walk in the door.

Creating Your Own High-Tech Resumes

Video Resumes

If you've decided to use a video resume, you should have a particular company—and preferably a specific position—in mind, says Vera Ehmann, owner of Career Advantage, a resume and career development service in Cambridge, Massachusetts. You also need to find out if your target company or companies will accept video resumes.

Once you've received a positive response, go ahead with creating the video. Call resume writing services or career counselors and ask if they produce video resumes. If they don't, they might be able to refer you to a video production company that has experience producing video resumes, or that at least specializes in business-related productions. The advantage of using a resume service is that you can also get valuable advice on what to discuss on the video. Do *not* simply try to produce your own videotape. A professional will be able to provide you with the proper lighting and equipment (and props, if necessary), as well as a high-quality tape.

Next you will need to write your script. Again, a resume writing service could help you with this aspect of production. According to Ehmann, video resumes work best when the video takes the shape of an interview where the subject is asked questions by an individual off-camera. The questions are fairly general, such as "What's your experience with marketing new products" or "What are your biggest strengths?" The questions should be open-ended so they allow you to discuss in-depth the information on your paper resume. In this respect, a video resume is more like an initial screening interview than an actual resume. Generally, you don't need to spell out your name, address, and phone number on the video; that information should be on the paper resume that you send along with the video. Of course, some people do include that information on the video, so it's your personal choice.

Ehmann also suggests creating a setting that is appropriate for whatever position you are applying for, such as a TV studio for a broadcasting position. Of course, a generic office setting is always appropriate. Be sure your attire is completely professional as well. Remember that your video will be the first chance you have to make an impression on a potential employer. Therefore, you should dress as you would for a first job interview—no jeans, T-shirts, or other casual dress.

Rehearse your script thoroughly. That way, you will appear less nervous and more natural and comfortable in front of the camera. As with a regular job interview, it is important to appear cool and confident. Be sure to speak clearly and slowly, and at the proper volume. You don't want to whisper, but you don't want to shout either. And of course, your video should be perfect, without flubbed lines, hesitations, or other mistakes. Don't try to liven up your video with flashy graphics or sound effects; your video should be simple and professional.

Once you have finished taping your resume, watch the tape carefully before sending it out to potential employers. Are you sitting up straight, looking directly at the camera? Do you have a pleasant, relaxed expression on your face? Does your voice sound confident and natural, not strained? If so, find a friend who will give you an honest opinion regarding your performance. When your video is up to par, it's time to send it out. And don't forget to include a paper copy of your resume; an employer will need this for their files, or to scan into their resume tracking system.

Multimedia Resumes

If you are planning on sending a multimedia resume on disk directly to a company, then, as with a video resume, you need to call the company to be sure that they have the capabilities to view it. When you call, you should also find out if the company primarily uses PCs or Macintosh computers. Of course, if you are planning on posting your resume online, or are planning on incorporating a resume onto your own Web page, then you will not need to do this. *For more information on posting your resume online, or creating your own Web page, see Chapter 2.*

If you are considering using a multimedia resume, you are probably already fairly knowledgeable about computers and have a sophisticated computer setup. Once you have the proper equipment, such as a sound card and scanner, you will need to decide how complicated you want to make your resume. After all, a cutting-edge multimedia resume won't do you any good if it requires such sophisticated equipment that few people would actually be able to use it. Therefore, your decision should be based upon your target audience. If you are in a nontechnical field, such as entertainment, you should try to design a multimedia resume that doesn't require all the best and latest computer equipment to view it. For a more technical position, such as a multimedia programmer, you can be more adventurous, while being relatively sure that the company you send your resume to will have the right equipment to access your resume. Keep in mind that the more uncomplicated the resume, the more people it will be available to. This advice holds true whether you are sending a resume on a disk, posting your resume online, or creating your own Web page.

Don't think that you need to be a computer whiz in order to create a good multimedia resume. If you have the basic equipment—and a reasonably good understanding of how computers work—your local bookstore or computer store has a number of different books that can teach you what you need to know. Depending on what you would like to accomplish, you may also need to buy some additional software for sound or graphics.

Once you understand how to design a multimedia resume, you need to determine what information you want to include. Most multimedia resumes include standard information, such as skills, experience, and accomplishments. Check out resumes posted online for ideas regarding design and content. Be creative when it comes to adding sound, graphics, or photographs! Use plenty of icons or menus to help guide users through your resume. After all, you can have a wonderfully imaginative resume, but if no one can figure out how to access your information, it will be worthless. One word of caution: Don't try to make your multimedia resume *too* flashy. Your graphics should enhance, not overshadow, your accomplishments.

After you complete your resume, go through it carefully for bugs, glitches, and other mistakes. Is all your information correct? Is spelling and punctuation correct? Are photographs, graphics, and sound clear? Can you easily access all parts of your resume? Once the answers to all these questions are "yes," ask a friend for a second opinion. It is important that a first-time user is able to easily navigate through your resume. Also, he or she might pick up some mistakes that your familiar eye didn't catch. Once your resume is complete, post it to the appropriate sites online or send it to a specific company (or companies). Again, be sure to include a paper version along with your disk.

In the future, job seekers may be able to produce their own video CD-ROMs. As CD-ROM technology becomes cheaper and more accessible, multimedia CD-ROMS will be an exciting way to market yourself to prospective employers. CD-ROM resumes will combine the power of both a video and multimedia resume, since video will be easily incorporated into a multimedia resume. And with a CD-ROM, sound, video, and graphics can be even more clear and sophisticated.

What You Need to Know Before You Use a Video or Multimedia Resume

For all the advantages of using an unconventional resume, there are a number of disadvantages as well, the biggest of which is the unconventionality of video and multimedia resumes. Video and multimedia resumes are far from common in the workplace for a number of reasons:

- **Time.** Human resources departments are increasingly short-staffed, as is evident in the increasing popularity of computer scanners to "read" resumes, applicant tracking systems, and computer-assisted job interviews. Most recruiters simply don't have time to spend more than five minutes on a new applicant, as is often required by these new, high-tech resumes.

- **Equipment.** Most recruiters don't have a VCR in their office, and many recruiters, especially those in nontechnical fields, don't have the right equipment to see and hear the information on multimedia resumes. If a company doesn't have the right equipment, your hard work could very well end up in the garbage.

- **Liability.** Many recruiters are fearful of using hiring methods where they could potentially be accused of allowing bias to color the selection process. Also, by conducting initial screening through video interviews, recruiters can open themselves up to potential lawsuits by virtue of age, race, gender, or weight discrimination—to name a few. Multimedia resumes are also susceptible to this problem, especially those that include personal information pertaining to age, marital status, or health, or a scanned photograph of the applicant.

At the same time, video and multimedia resumes *are* appropriate in certain fields and situations. And even in fields where they are not commonplace, video and multimedia resumes can be an unusual and effective way to get noticed. In either case, however, you should call the company to verify that they accept video or multimedia resumes. Most importantly, your video or multimedia presentation should be *unparalleled* in quality! After all, if recruiters take the time to look at your special resume, you'd better make sure it's worth their while.

PART TWO

FINDING ADVERTISED JOBS THE ELECTRONIC WAY

CHAPTER FOUR

COMMERCIAL ONLINE SERVICES

Commercial online services offer job hunters a full range of career services, including networking resources, areas to post resumes, business databases for researching companies, and finally, job listings. This chapter will explore some of the available resources for job listings on four major commercial online services: **America Online**, **CompuServe**, **The Microsoft Network**, and **Prodigy**. We'll also touch briefly on two of the smaller services in Delphi and GEnie. And because many services provide their users with valuable, comprehensive career resources that do not include job listings, we have included those resources in this chapter as well. *However, resources devoted exclusively to resume posting, company research, and networking are described in their respective chapters.*

An Introduction to Commercial Online Services

Unlike the terms "Usenet" or "World Wide Web," which refer to specific areas of the Internet, the phrase "commercial online service" is used to describe **a company that charges a fee for access to its online services.** While this may sound just like an Internet service provider, there's an important difference: Internet service providers allow users to access different areas of the

Internet, like Usenet or the Web. Commercial online services do this as well, but also provide access to their own resources—services that were developed especially for their subscribers.

During the 1980s, the period when most commercial services were being developed and introduced, the Internet was largely an arena for a select group of academics, scientists, and government officials. Unless you were in one of these groups, it was nearly impossible to secure Internet access. Usenet newsgroups were used mainly by computer scientists and other intellectuals, and the Web was still years away from being a reality. **Commercial online services were developed in order to bring online services to the masses.** These services quickly became popular because of the information and entertainment they provided—such as up-to-the minute stock quotes and interactive games. Plus, their colorful, graphic user interfaces made commercial services easy to navigate, even for users with little computer experience.

Today, commercial services remain a favorite of families and—to a lesser extent—businesses. Services like CompuServe are often the easiest way to learn about cyberspace. Many people, especially technical neophytes, find commercial online services less intimidating to use than the Internet. Unlike the Internet, for instance, the information on online services is well-organized and easy to find. Additionally, new users can take advantage of online tutorials and guided tours that teach new members how to use the service most effectively. Also, most services have an online member support area where users can find answers to many frequently asked questions. If they can't find an answer, they can leave a question for a member services representative. The Internet simply does not have these types of support systems for its users, which is a main reason why more than thirteen million users rely on commercial online services as their main source for online information.

The Good and the Bad News about Commercial Online Services

While the major commercial online services share a common history and purpose, and have many similarities, no two services are exactly alike. For instance, Delphi began as a text-based service without any graphics or art, while America Online relies heavily on art to enhance its service. Not all differences, however, are as marked as that. Many are different simply in terms of the services they offer. For instance, some are more entertainment-oriented while others are more business-oriented.

If you are considering subscribing to a commercial online service, you probably already have a good sense of what you are looking for in a service, whether it be entertainment, information, or easy Web access. The following is simply an overview of each service to indicate its relative strengths and weaknesses. To find out more information on how to sign up with a commercial online service, call the phone numbers listed. In most cases, you will receive free software that will let you try out the service free for one month. Be careful! In the case of at least one service, that free month is a *calendar* month, and if you sign up on July 24th, for example, you'll actually only get one *week* free. So be sure to ask.

- **America Online, 800-827-6364.** The largest commercial online service with nearly nine million subscribers, America Online is well-known for its wide range of home and leisure activities for the entire family. Since the creation of the online Career Center in 1989, America Online has been the leader among commercial online services in terms of the resources it offers for job hunters. America Online's employment databases contain a total of almost 30,000 job openings, and all use the same fairly simple search engine to access information in the databases. With the exception of the online newspapers and federal employment opportunities, these job listings can all be accessed with the keyword "Help Wanted." Then, you merely need to pick the appropriate site from the Careers main menu. If you decide to use AOL, be sure to upgrade to the 3.0 version. Otherwise, every time you enter a new area on AOL, you must wait for what seems like an eternity while AOL downloads new art (even with a 28.8 modem). In the 3.0 version, however, all the art is downloaded during installation.

- **CompuServe, 800-848-8199.** A large portion of CompuServe's four and a half million subscribers are businesses, which is a good indication of the service's orientation. CompuServe has by far the best collection of business resources available online, including dozens of business-related databases. Job listings are not the primary reason most job hunters like using CompuServe. While it does have two services devoted to job listings, CompuServe Classifieds and E-Span, its strengths lie in its research capabilities and professional forums, which are discussed in depth in Chapters 11 and 12, respectively. And of course, CompuServe offers subscribers complete Internet access, including a Web browser, so subscribers can also access career-related newsgroups and Web sites. Another CompuServe strength is its forums—over 900 special groups for people of like ideas and interests to gather and exchange information.

- **The Microsoft Network, 800-386-5550.** Known the world over for its personal computer software, Microsoft got off to a late start in the commercial online services game and has been playing catch-up throughout the mid-'90s. The popularity of the company's Windows 95 operating system has been helping The Microsoft Network (MSN) draw new subscribers, however, and it's a safe bet that Microsoft will soon be a major player in the services scene. For the moment, members will want to check out its Career Forum, which features a wealth of job search and career advice, tutorials, and information. Specialized forums include ones devoted to nursing and theatre professions, and The Mining Company offers career information and links to other educational sites.

- **Prodigy, 800-776-3449.** In the past, Prodigy was best known as the favorite online service of families with young children, mainly because of its educational resources and games. But today, Prodigy's greatest asset is the easy Internet access it provides for its subscribers. Users can easily switch between Prodigy's services, the Web, Usenet newsgroups, and Gopher. Plus, Prodigy's main menu even contains some hypertext links to Prodigy-sponsored Web sites. One important note: Prodigy has recently divided its services into *Prodigy Classic*, which offers an impressive variety of member services, and *Prodigy Internet*, which is distinguished primarily by its faster and more complete access to the Internet, via a partnership with Microsoft's Internet Explorer. You'll need Prodigy Classic to access the career resources on the following pages, which include a strong collection of regional listings with employment classifieds from *Newsday* and the *Richmond Times-Dispatch*. And Prodigy's Career Connections is an excellent example of the service's ability to incorporate the World Wide Web into a traditional online service.

In addition to these major services, the following two services are worth mentioning here—if for no other reason than that they were once somewhat more prominent than they are today. They are as follows:

- **Delphi, 800-695-4005.** Delphi is currently accessible either on the World Wide Web (**www.delphi.com**) or as a dial-up, text-only service. There are a variety of membership plans available, including free access to its various forums. Delphi's text-only service looks much like one of the Bulletin Board Systems described in Chapter 8, and offers full Internet access, including an excellent newsgroup reader. Delphi offers relatively little in the way of career resources, although there are a few special interest groups that are useful for networking (*see Chapter 12*).

- **GEnie, 800-638-9636.** Another small service (less than 20,000 subscribers), GEnie is a hybrid of a text-based service like Delphi and a graphical, easy-to-use service like America Online. For instance, GEnie's opening screen uses icons, but all the individual services are text-only, which makes it fairly difficult to navigate at times. While GEnie offers access to the entire Internet, including the World Wide Web, it uses a text-based Web browser so you only receive the text portions of a Web site. GEnie does have several career-related services in operation at the time of this writing.

At one time, not all commercial online services provided subscribers with full Internet access. Commercial online services and the Internet were seen as two separate and opposing services; you either used one or the other, but not both. But, as you will see in Chapter 6, the World Wide Web has opened the Internet to the general population, and today, all the major services offer complete Internet and Web access.

Another characteristic these services have in common is cost, which is traditionally the biggest drawback of commercial online services. Most commercial services recruit new members by giving away trial memberships. Services often waive their monthly fee for one month (be sure to check on specifics!), and offer up to ten free hours of connect time. If you exceed those free hours, though, you'll be assessed the regular hourly charge, usually about $2–$4. And of course, as soon as that free trial period is up, you immediately begin assessing charges, which can pile up quickly. The monthly membership fee is usually around $10, or more for unlimited usage. Plus, many commercial services charge additional fees for entering certain areas or accessing databases, such as CompuServe's Dun & Bradstreet's business databases.

Today, most commercial online services offer plans which provide customers with unlimited access, generally for about $19.95 a month. (GEnie is one exception to this rule, charging a subscription fee of approximately $24, plus an hourly fee after a certain number of hours per month. Unlike the other services, GEnie does not offer a free trial period, and applies a surcharge for daytime use.) America Online's switch of most of its customers over to unlimited usage in late 1996 led to a public relations nightmare that the company was still trying to live down in mid-1997; the new freedom proved so attractive to customers that many users couldn't get through a busy signal to enjoy the service. Still, the increasing popularity of the World Wide Web has made unlimited plans a sensible choice for many customers.

One note: there may well be a financial benefit to eschewing commercial online services altogether in favor of a direct Internet connection. The primary advantage is that you pay only a monthly service charge to your Internet service provider—all your time spent online (provided you have a local access telephone number) costs only as much as a local phone call. Check for providers in your area, keeping in mind that you'll miss out on the member services detailed on the next few pages.

Where to Find Job Listings and Other Career Resources

As stated before, the major commercial online resources offer a wealth of information on a wide variety of subjects. Among the information you'll find on these services are: online versions of popular magazines; up-to-the-minute news and financial information; online malls where you can shop at nationally known retail stores; discussion and interest groups dedicated to hundreds of different special interest groups; and entire volumes of encyclopedias. You can also make plane or hotel reservations, find information on different cities and restaurants, download cutting-edge software, and of course, uncover thousands of hidden job listings.

However, the job listings found on commercial online services are nowhere near as extensive as those found through Usenet newsgroups or the World Wide Web. For example, Usenet has over 90,000 job listings in their newsgroups, while the Web site America's Job Bank contains more than 250,000 jobs in its database. The largest database on a commercial online service at the time of this writing is America Online's Help Wanted USA, at 11,000 listings. At the same time, numbers aren't everything, and most of the job listing sites described on the following pages are well worth a visit. Additionally, all five of the commercial services mentioned provide access to Usenet and the Web, which means that users can browse those job databases as well. America Online, for one, offers links to a number of major job hunting sites on the World Wide Web through its own sites. *Such sites will be covered in detail in Chapter 6. The purpose of the following pages is to cover those sites which are offered exclusively by commercial online services.*

In the listings that follow, you will find the name of the resource, followed by the **Keyword** that's necessary in order to access the resource. Each service calls its keyword something different. In America Online, it's "keyword"; in CompuServe, Delphi, and The Microsoft Network, it's "go"; in GEnie, you "move to" a specific page number; and in Prodigy, it's "jump to." The **Number of job listings** is rounded down; for instance, if a site had 503 job listings, we said 500; if a site had 11,128 listings, we rounded that down to 11,000. When we were unable to determine information with a reasonable degree of accuracy, N/A was used. **Types of jobs** indicates in general terms what fields or job categories you are likely to find job listings for; similarly, **Locations of jobs** indicates for what countries, states, or cities job listings can be found. **Frequency of updates** indicates how often job listings are added to the database. **Search criteria available** shows you how the database can be searched. Most sites allow you to search by some combination of job category, location, company, or keywords; some let you search only by keyword. And the **Insider tips** section is a general overview of a service and its special features, along with helpful tips for the insider. For services without job listings, we have simply furnished the name of the resource, keyword, and an overview of the service and the resources provided.

AOL CLASSIFIEDS/ EMPLOYMENT AD BOARDS

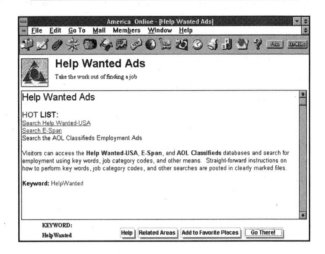

Keyword: Classifieds

Number of job listings: 3,600

Types of jobs: Administrative, engineering, executive, legal, health, and social services

Locations of jobs: United States

Frequency of updates: Daily

Search criteria available: Job category

Insider tips: When most job hunters think of America Online and job listings, they immediately turn to Help Wanted USA. However, the lesser-known AOL Classifieds contains thousands of job listings that are *not* available in Help Wanted USA, or anywhere else for that matter, and are well worth a look. This site can be reached in a number of different ways, including by simply going to "Find on AOL." These ads are posted by America Online members and change regularly. They can be accessed through AOL's Careers page (keyword: Careers) although they are not part of that service. One note: Most ads do not include a street address, and require job hunters to respond to all postings through email.

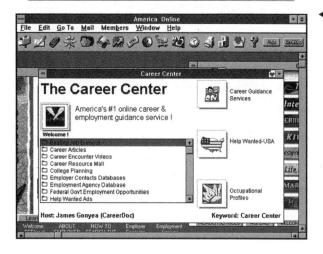

Keyword: Career Center

America Online's Career Center is a comprehensive employment guide with an exhaustive library of resources for job hunters. It is one of the oldest and finest job hunting sites that can be found anywhere online. Through the Career Center, job hunters can access job listings such as Help Wanted USA, or Talent Bank, the resume database run by Gonyea and Associates. Other key features include:

- *Career Guidance.* Includes workbook exercises to help job hunters find a satisfying career and drop-in sessions with career counselors to find answers to user's career questions.
- *Career Resources Mall.* An online mall where job hunters can purchase career-related merchandise.
- *Internship Opportunities Directory.* Contains information for thousands of paid and unpaid internships.
- *Job Hunting Advice.* Includes tips on networking, negotiating a salary or raise, and retirement planning. Job hunters will also find resume and cover letter templates, and advice on how to write a keyword resume.
- *Occupational Profiles.* Contains 250 detailed profiles of popular occupations taken from the U.S. Department of Labor publication, the *Occupational Outlook Handbook*. Users will also find a list of "hot jobs," those positions that are expected to experience higher than average growth within the next ten years.

CHICAGO TRIBUNE
CLASSIFIEDS

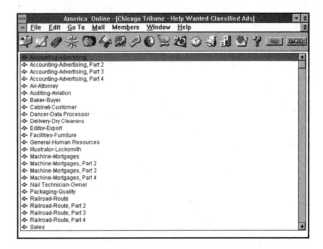

Keyword: Trib Ads

Number of job listings: 1,500

Types of jobs: All, including accounting, sales, computers, and health care

Locations of jobs: Chicago, Illinois and vicinity

Frequency of updates: Weekly

Search criteria available: Keyword or job code category. You can also browse the listings alphabetically.

Insider tips: If you live in the Chicago area or are interested in relocating there, then this is a must-see. The employment classifieds are taken straight from the Sunday *Tribune*, which is the largest collection of help-wanted advertisements in the region. To make it easier for job hunters, the classifieds are divided into three categories: general help wanted, health care, and technical. You can search each smaller category or search the entire database. One note: The classifieds sections from several other newspapers, including *The New York Times* and *The Orlando Sentinel*, are also available through America Online.

FEDERAL GOVERNMENT
EMPLOYMENT OPPORTUNITIES

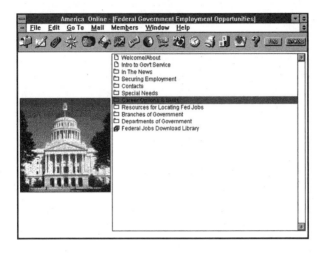

Keyword: Career Center (Choose "Federal Career Opportunities")

Number of job listings: 2,200

Types of jobs: All, including accounting, administrative, financial, technical

Locations of jobs: United States and its territories

Frequency of updates: Weekly

Search criteria available: Geographic location

Insider tips: These job openings from the United States Office of Personnel Management are obtained each week by Gonyea and Associates, the same company that assembles the Help Wanted USA jobs database. These listings are not presented as a searchable database; instead, you can find them in a number of separate downloadable text files, such as Fed Jobs/Northeastern and Fed Jobs/Overseas/Pacific. In order to view the listings, you must download them and then read them through your word processing program or text editor. Unfortunately, the job listings give you little information besides job title and contact information. You can also find an index of federal occupations, where to find other resources for federal job openings, information regarding civil service exams, instructions on how to apply for a federal job, and information on the three branches of government.

HELP WANTED USA

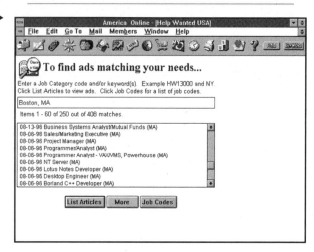

Keyword: Help Wanted (Choose "Job Listings" and then "Career Center's Help Wanted Ads")

Number of job listings: 11,000

Types of jobs: All, including administrative, education, financial, management, medical, and technical

Locations of jobs: United States and Canada

Frequency of updates: Weekly

Search criteria available: Job category and keyword

Insider tips: One of the most comprehensive collections of job listings found online, Help Wanted USA is a must-see for anyone with access to America Online. You can find openings for all fields and experience levels, and the job listings themselves are extensive and detailed. There's a link to About Work, which features loads of career advice, interviews with career professionals, and other job hunting services. There are also links from this site to other job search areas on America Online and the World Wide Web. Help Wanted USA is a service of James Gonyea and Associates, pioneers in the world of online career services, and the people behind America Online's Career Center.

COMPUSERVE CLASSIFIEDS

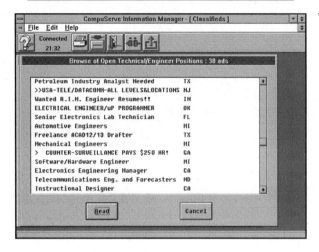

Go: classifieds

Number of job listings: 100

Types of jobs: Technical/engineering, marketing/sales, computers, and others

Locations of jobs: United States, Canada, and the United Kingdom

Frequency of updates: Daily

Search criteria available: Job category

Insider tips: The quality of postings in this database varies greatly. While the majority of listings are genuine employment opportunities, many are the sketchy "make money quick" or "I'm making a fortune at home" variety. The true job listings, however, are for job hunters of all levels, and include both permanent full-time and contract work. Look for job listings under "Positions Open." The classifieds also have space to post jobs and positions wanted. One note: When the previous edition of this book was produced, there were more than 400 job listings available at this site. At the time of this writing, there were barely 100, and many of those were the aforementioned "Get rich on the Internet" type. It's difficult to say whether the job figures of one year ago will be approached in the future.

E-SPAN JOB LISTINGS

Go: espan

Number of job listings: 10,000

Types of jobs: All, including banking, computers, financial, media, entertainment, science, and medical

Locations of jobs: United States, Canada, the United Kingdom, and other international locations

Frequency of updates: Daily

Search criteria available: Job category and geographic location

Insider tips: The CompuServe version of the popular job hunting World Wide Web site has more features than the version once available on America Online, but still lacks the resume database and employer profiles of the Web version. But the CompuServe site does offer some important job hunting information, like networking and interviewing tips, as well as rules and advice for writing resumes. The jobs database is divided into 17 different categories ("Internet Related Services", "Business Services/Investments", etc.) to make your job search easier.

E-SPAN CAREER MANAGEMENT FORUM

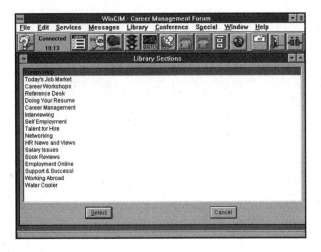

Go: careers

Not to be confused with E-Span's job listings site, the Career Management Forum provides an outlet for job hunters from all fields and experience levels to exchange career-related advice, information, and tips. The forum is structured like other CompuServe professional forums, with areas for job hunters to post messages, participate in real-time chats, or look up files in the library. There are sixteen career topics covered, including resume writing, networking, today's job market, career management, salaries, finding employment online, and working abroad. You can, for instance, submit your resume for critique, or post questions like, "How do you discuss being fired during a job interview?" There's even a section for job hunters to give and receive support during what is often an extremely stressful period of their lives. There are also special appearances by nationally recognized career counselors and various professionals specializing in providing job search advice.

GENERAL BUSINESS FORUM

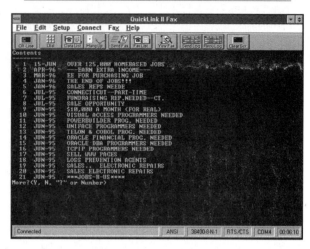

(Choose "Employment Opportunities" from the Classifieds
Menu)

Number of job listings: 100

Types of jobs: Computers, clerical, and sales

Locations of jobs: United States

Frequency of updates: Sporadic

Search criteria available: None.

Insider tips: Delphi's employment classifieds are fairly limited
in number, and contain some job listings that are almost six
months old. For this reason, you may be better off
selecting "Usenet Newsgroups" from the main menu and
exploring the opportunities available through the job-
related newsgroups.

THE JOB COMPLEX

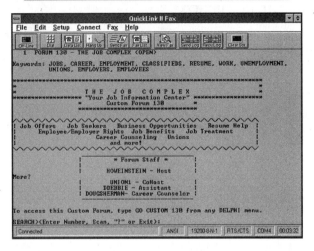

Go: CUSTOM 130

The Job Complex is Delphi's answer to America Online's Career Center and CompuServe's Career Management Forum. In it, job hunters will find advice and tips on a wide range of job hunting topics, such as preparing resumes, networking, and job interviewing. The Job Complex also includes information on common job benefits offered, trade unions, and more. The forum section is a place where users can exchange information and advice with each other, as well as post job hunting and career-related questions to experts from JobBank USA. There's also a place for "situations wanted" postings, and budding entrepreneurs can find listings of new business ventures.

THE BUSINESS RESOURCE DIRECTORY

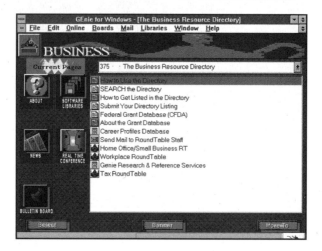

Move to: 375

> This directory has a number of different resources available for job hunters and small business owners. The Business Resource Directory itself has information on thousands of businesses and services available nationwide. Each listing contains the name, address, and phone number of the business or service, as well as a brief description. The database is searchable by keywords so job hunters can pinpoint the exact information they are looking for. Users can also access a federal grants database, which is a directory of all federal research grants available, as well as the Home Office/Small Business Owners Round Table, a discussion group for the growing number of people who work from home or own their own business.

CAREER PROFILES
DATABASE

```
GEnie for Windows - [Terminal Window]
 File  Edit  Online  Boards  Mail  Libraries  Window  Help

            Echo On
            BS/DEL

Medical Assistants

950114
<D.O.T. 078.361-038 and .364-014; 079.362-010, .364-010,
and -014, and .374-018; 355.662-010>

Nature of the Work
     Medical assistants perform routine clinical and clerical

tasks to keep offices of physicians, podiatrists,
chiropractors, and optometrists running smoothly. Medical
assistants should not be confused with physician assistants,
who examine, diagnose, and treat patients, under the direct
supervision of a physician. Physician assistants are
discussed elsewhere in the Handbook.

     The duties of medical assistants vary from office to
office, depending on office location, size, and specialty.
In small practices, medical assistants are usually
generalists, handling both clerical and clinical duties
and reporting directly to an office manager, physician, or
other health practitioner. Those in large practices tend to
```

Move to: 1411

> Compiled from the U.S. Department of Labor's
> *Occupational Outlook Handbook*, GEnie's Career Profiles
> Database contains detailed information on 250 common
> occupations. This is an especially useful resource for job
> hunters contemplating a career change or for college
> students and recent graduates still trying to decide on a
> career path. Among other features, the database contains
> information on training and education requirements, typical
> duties, salaries, and the job outlook for a particular
> occupation.

DR. JOB

```
GEnie for Windows - [Terminal Window]
 File  Edit  Online  Boards  Mail  Libraries  Window  Help

    ☒ Echo On
    ☒ BS/DEL
                        Dr. Job Career Tips
 1.  Finding Job for the Military  (960822)
 2.  How to reduce job stress  (960814)
 3.  No guts no glory in jobs too  (960808)
 4.  30-year-old wins top spot on Chicago convention Committee  (960801)
 5.  If you can figure, figure on a good third quarter  (960724)
 6.  What employers look for  (960718)
 7.  Health problems go to court  (960618)
 8.  Menopause is new problem in career path  (960618)
 9.  Revitalizing your workplace  (960618)
10.  How executives should act on new job  (960618)
11.  More execs choosing parent track  (960612)
12.  Kraft supermoms take families up career ladder  (960605)
13.  Companies seeking workers with moxie  (960530)
14.  Who's whistling while they work?  (960522)
15.  Family relationships affect your work  (960516)

Item #, or <RETURN> for more?
```

Move to: 395

Dr. Job dispenses advice covering a wide range of career and employment issues, such as networking, staying motivated during a job hunt, and coping with competition on the job. The column, which is in a question and answer format, is updated once a week, and users can post questions to Dr. Job that will either be answered personally or through the column. Dr. Job also maintains a library of old columns so job hunters can search for topics of special interest to them.

GENIE RESEARCH AND REFERENCE SERVICES

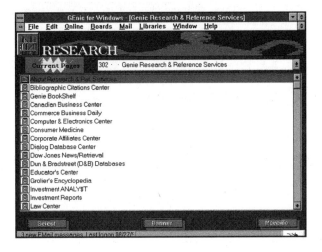

Move to: 302

> This is a list of resources available through GEnie for
> researching companies and industries, and finding career-
> related information. One of the many services found here
> is GEnie's newsstand, where job hunters can conduct full-
> text searches of the *Los Angeles Times, Chicago Tribune,
> Boston Globe*, and other newspapers. Job hunters can also
> access several business databases, such as the Thomas
> Register, Dialog Database Center, and Dun & Bradstreet,
> where they can find comprehensive information on
> thousands of companies, as well as general industry
> information. Users who access these and other resources
> through this service will incur fees—usually of about $5—in
> addition to the regular GEnie connect-time charges.

CAREER CONNECTIONS!

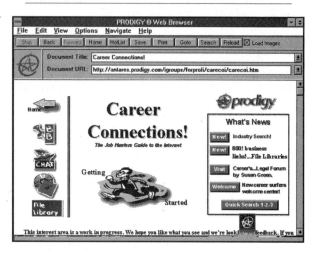

Jump to: career connections

Career Connections! seems to be Prodigy's answer to America Online's Career Center, except that it's written in hypertext, so it has links to dozens of other career sites on the Web. It has plenty of valuable information to offer to job hunters. Among the resources you'll find here:

- *Quick Search 1-2-3.* Allows job hunters to perform keyword searches in three of the Web's major job hunting sites, the Monster Board, the Online Career Center, and Career Mosaic, as well as job-related Usenet newsgroups, thus exposing users to over 100,000 job listings!
- *Industry Search.* Links to six different industry-specific job searching sites, including MedSearch America and FedWorld.
- *Resume Connections.* Provides five different resume templates for users to write their own resumes.
- *The Career Travel Guide.* Links to many of the World Wide Web's biggest career sites, such as CareerCity.
- *Message Board and Chat Area.* Allows job hunters to exchange job hunting advice and ideas.
- *File Library.* Includes hundreds of career-related files, including 800 links to business-related sites, as well as job hunting tips on writing resumes and cover letters, networking, contacting companies, interviewing, and more.

GATEWAY VIRGINIA

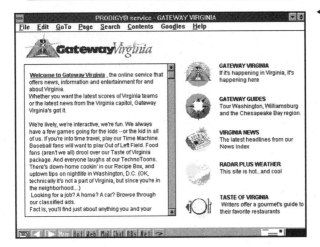

Jump to: gateway virginia
Number of job listings: 1,500
Types of jobs: All
Locations of jobs: Virginia, with a focus on the Richmond area
Frequency of updates: Daily
Search criteria available: Must browse listings alphabetically
Insider tips: Employment ads from the daily and Sunday
Richmond Times-Dispatch and other Virginia publications.
This free resource also has extensive information about the
Richmond area, including a guided tour of the Shenandoah
Valley. There is also information available from a variety of
news sources, including the Virginia News Network and
the Virginia Associated Press Wire.

NEWSDAY

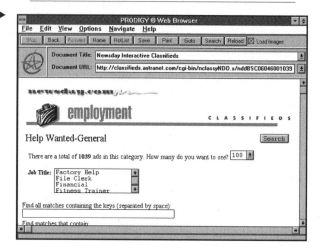

Jump to: newsday

Number of job listings: 1,000

Types of jobs: All, including professional, technical, administrative, and blue collar

Locations of jobs: Long Island, New York

Frequency of updates: Daily

Search criteria available: Job titles and keywords

Insider tips: Users can find employment classifieds from New York's *Newsday* newspaper, the largest paper on Long Island. Plus, users can scan the online version of *Newsday* for information about local companies and industries.

ONLINE CLASSIFIEDS

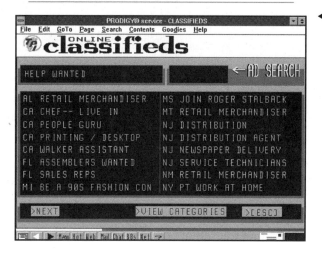

Jump to: classifieds

Number of job listings: 25

Types of jobs: All, including retail, sales, marketing, and computers

Locations of jobs: United States

Frequency of updates: Daily

Search criteria available: None

Insider tips: The online classifieds also has areas for the posting of positions wanted and business opportunities. But this is the weak link of Prodigy's career services. It's worth a glance every once in a while, but with so many other excellent resources available, we recommend that you don't spend too much time here.

TAMPA BAY ONLINE

Jump to: tampa bay online

Number of job listings: 1,500

Types of jobs: All, including professional, technical, health care, clerical, and full- or part-time

Locations of jobs: Tampa Bay and surrounding areas

Frequency of updates: Daily

Search criteria available: Category, job title, and location

Insider tips: Another regional employment listing, this one is from the *Tampa Bay Tribune* employment classifieds. It includes a link to the *Tribune* Web page, where you can find valuable news and information about Florida. One note: As of late 1997, Tampa Bay Online was a Prodigy Custom Choice, with membership enrollment required.

USENET NEWSGROUPS

senet newsgroups are one of the oldest and most misunderstood areas of the Internet. What was once the exclusive territory of this country's brain trust—academics, scientists, and top government officials—has developed into one of the most popular means of exchanging information on the Internet. At the same time, many new users are scared off by what they perceive as an intimidating Usenet culture. But by ignoring the discussion groups on Usenet, you could miss out on hundreds of potential job opportunities.

How Usenet Newsgroups Are Structured

Quite simply, Usenet is a collection of thousands of individual discussion groups, called newsgroups, which can be accessed through a direct Internet connection or through commercial online services like America Online or CompuServe. Usenet allows millions of users worldwide to discuss any topic imaginable—anarchy, current events, Elvis—you name it. Because newsgroups cover such a wide range of topics, they are broken down by hierarchies, or general categories, which enable you to more easily find the topics you want. The main hierarchies are as follows:

alt. (alternative)
comp. (computers)

misc. (miscellaneous)
news. (news for Usenet users)
rec. (recreation)
sci. (science)
soc. (social issues)
talk. (serious discussions about often controversial
issues)

There are also dozens of local hierarchies, such as atl. (Atlanta), il. (Illinois), or swnet. (Sweden), which don't fall into any of the above hierarchies. The local hierarchies have newsgroups that cover subjects like city politics, and some are online classifieds, with objects like cars, bicycles, or kittens up for sale.

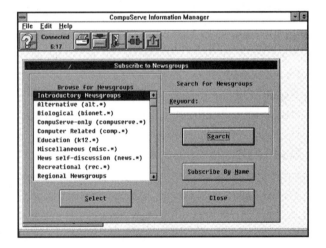

Newsgroups can be further broken down according to subject. For instance, **alt.backrubs** is in the alternative hierarchy under the subject "backrubs." And they can get even more specialized: **alt.movies.hitchcock** and **alt.movies.monster** are in the alternative hierarchy, under the general subject "movies," discussing the movies of Alfred Hitchcock and the monster genre, respectively. Finally, each newsgroup contains discussion threads, which are basically a group of messages relating to the same topic. Every time someone posts a message regarding a new topic, a new thread is started.

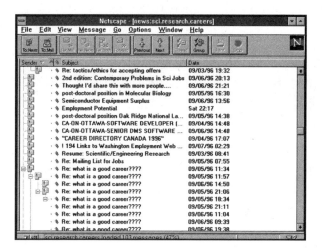

Ironically, it is this organizational and hierarchal structure that turns many people off to newsgroups. Many people open their newsreader to find a list of newsgroups, with directories and sub-directories of subdirectories, and immediately close it back up, simply because they are intimidated by what they see. They decide it's simply not worth it for them to figure out how the whole thing works, so they'll just stick with their commercial services and the World Wide Web. Unfortunately, they are missing out on a real jewel of the Internet.

How to Get Started in Newsgroups

As mentioned earlier, Usenet newsgroups are accessible either through your Internet carrier or through commercial online ser-vices. Try Keyword: Newsgroups in AOL. **If you have a regular Internet connection, you will need the help of a newsreader, such as Trumpet Newsreader, to actually read the messages in newsgroups.** A newsreader simply organizes the thousands of available newsgroups, and allows you to read and post messages. Many Web browsers, like Netscape Navigator, have a built-in newsreader. Netscape's newsreader is called simply Netscape News. If you can't find a newsreader on your system, call your Internet provider and ask where to find one.

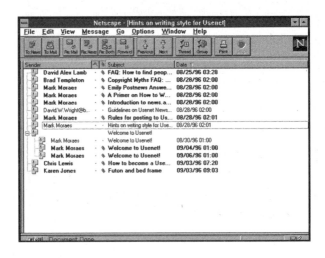

Once you're in Usenet, you should read the messages in the newsgroups **news.newusers.questions** and **news.announce.newusers**. In these newsgroups, you'll find answers to the most commonly asked questions regarding Usenet, or you can post your own questions about Usenet. You can also find information such as a history of the Internet, rules for posting messages, and hints about the Usenet writing style.

After reviewing the basics of Usenet, post a test message to the newsgroups **alt.test** or **misc.tests**. This test simply allows you to check whether your newsreader is configured properly. If you cannot post test messages, ask your Internet carrier or commercial service provider for assistance.

If your test goes off without a hitch, then you are all set. But before you begin posting messages to dozens of newsgroups on the Web, there are a few basic facts about Usenet you need to know. First, different hierarchies and newsgroups have different tones to their discussions. In general, alt. newsgroups are more casual, while the comp. and sci. newsgroups are more formal and factual. And talk. newsgroups discuss serious subjects in a serious manner. It's important to take the time—at least one week—to get a feel for a newsgroup. This can usually be done simply by reading a few days' worth of messages. Doing this should decrease your chances of posting an inappropriate message. *For a more complete discussion on the do's and don'ts of newsgroups, or "netiquette," be sure to read Chapter 12, Networking Online. This chapter will explain in more detail the intricacies of the Usenet culture.*

Using Usenet to Find Jobs

Besides being an outlet for discussions on topics as serious as politics and as frivolous as Barry Manilow, Usenet newsgroups are also one of the best sources on the Internet for job listings. In addition to the resume newsgroups mentioned in Chapter 2, Usenet has over one hundred newsgroups dedicated to job postings, each containing dozens, and often hundreds, of job listings. Some national newsgroups can even contain thousands of different job listings!

You can use job-related newsgroups to look for full-time and part-time positions, as well as short-term, contract, freelance, or consulting work. In fact, there are a number of newsgroups dedicated to postings for contractual labor. **The majority of job-related newsgroups are local, but you can find plenty of national ones as well.** At the time of this writing, though, most of the newsgroups researched for this book had a heavy emphasis on high-tech positions, like computers and engineering. However, this is not to say that you will not find postings for accountants or secretaries. But job hunters in less technical fields may need to look a little more carefully to find postings appropriate to their fields.

Because so many newsgroups are local and targeted toward a specific region, they are an excellent resource for job hunters interested in relocating. If you're interested in moving to another city or even another country, you can get a feel for the job market and send out your resume, without the cost of a subscription to an out-of-town newspaper.

Newsgroup job listings are also valuable because they contain more information than a traditional newspaper help-wanted advertisement. In general, these advertisements spell out the requirements for and duties of the position in great detail. One big reason for this is cost—employers, employment agencies, and professional recruiters can post job listings for free, regardless of how large or small the listing is. Few other job listing resources, whether on the Internet or in print, can say the same.

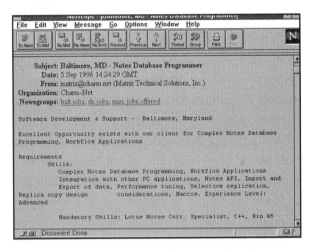

How to Instantly Search Many Newsgroups

Many of the larger job-hunting Web sites, such as CareerCity (**http://www.careercity.com**) or CareerMosaic (**http://www. careermosaic.com**), provide a search engine that allows you to simultaneously search more than 100 employment newsgroups for job openings. With one search on CareerCity, for example, you can instantly hunt through over 100,000 Usenet job openings by newsgroup or by keyword. For that matter, many search engines enable you to conduct searches on the World Wide Web *or* Usenet, and Deja News (**http://www.dejanews.com**) is an excellent search mechanism in its own right. Deja News allows searches by specific topic, and has an extensive classifieds section.

Major Job Posting Newsgroups

The newsgroups listed here are specifically for the posting of jobs, but you can often find one or two job postings in a newsgroup related to your profession, so you should try to check in fairly regularly with those types of groups. For instance, if you're a veterinarian, drop in on **alt.med.veterinary**, just in case something turns up.

One note of caution: Beware of job postings that sound too good to be true. A number of sites contain job postings with subjects along the lines of "$$MAKE MONEY AT HOME!$$" Our advice is to stay clear of those types of postings. Unfortunately, on Usenet as in real life, there are a number of unscrupulous characters who try to make money off of desperate people who are looking for work. Therefore, don't believe that simply because a job is posted on the Internet, it's legitimate.

The following list is designed to help you find job openings in your particular region or field. It should also be noted that each individual Internet provider and online service decides which newsgroups to carry; therefore, not all newsgroups will be available to everyone.

NORTHEAST/MID-ATLANTIC

balt.jobs
Jobs available in Baltimore, Maryland.

conn.jobs.offered
Jobs available in Connecticut.

dc.jobs
Employment opportunities in Washington, DC.

ithaca.jobs
Job opportunities in the Ithaca, New York area.

li.jobs
Jobs available on Long Island, New York.

md.jobs
Jobs available in Maryland and Washington, DC.

me.jobs
Jobs available in Maine.

ne.jobs
Employment opportunities in New England.

ne.jobs.contract
Contract labor in New England.

niagara.jobs
Jobs available in the Niagara region of New York.

nj.wanted
Employment opportunities in New Jersey.

nyc.jobs
Employment opportunities in New York City.

nyc.jobs.contract
Contract labor and consulting opportunities in
    New York City.

nyc.jobs.offered
More jobs available in New York City.

pgh.jobs.offered
Jobs available in the Pittsburgh, Pennsylvania area.

phl.jobs.offered
Job opportunities in Philadelphia, Pennsylvania.

SOUTHEAST
atl.jobs
Employment opportunities in and around Atlanta, Georgia.

fl.jobs
Job opportunities in Florida.

hsv.jobs
Jobs available in Huntsville, Alabama.

lou.lft.jobs
Employment opportunities in the Lafayette, Louisiana area.

memphis.employment
Employment opportunities in the Memphis, Tennessee area.

tnn.jobs
Professional job opportunities in Tennessee.

triangle.jobs
Jobs available in the Research Triangle of Raleigh, Durham, and
    Chapel Hill, North Carolina.

uark.jobs
Jobs wanted and available at the University of Arkansas.

us.sc.columbia.employment
Jobs available at the University of South Carolina at Columbia.

va.jobs
Job opportunities in Virginia.

MIDWEST

chi.jobs
Jobs available in the Chicago, Illinois area.

cle.jobs
Jobs available in the Cleveland, Ohio area.

cmh.jobs
Job opportunities in Columbus, Ohio.

il.jobs.offered
Employment opportunities in Illinois.

in.jobs
Job opportunities in Indianapolis, Indiana.

mi.jobs
Jobs available in Michigan.

milw.jobs
Jobs available in the Milwaukee, Wisconsin area.

mn.jobs
Employment opportunities in Minnesota.

oh.jobs
Jobs available and wanted in Ohio.

stl.jobs
Jobs available in St. Louis, Missouri.

umn.general.jobs
Jobs available at the University of Minnesota.

WEST/SOUTHWEST

austin.jobs
Jobs available in Austin, Texas.

az.jobs
Jobs available in Arizona.

ba.jobs.contract
Contract labor in the San Francisco Bay area, California.

ba.jobs.offered
Full-time employment opportunities in the San Francisco Bay
    area, California.

co.jobs
Jobs available in Colorado.

dfw.jobs
Jobs available in Dallas/Ft. Worth, Texas.

houston.jobs.offered
Jobs available in Houston, Texas.

la.jobs
Jobs available in Los Angeles, Ventura, and Orange Counties,
    California.

nm.jobs
Jobs available in New Mexico.

nv.jobs
Job opportunities in Nevada.

pdaxs.jobs.computers
Computer-related job opportunities in Portland, Oregon.

pdaxs.jobs.engineering
Engineering and technical job opportunities in Portland, Oregon.

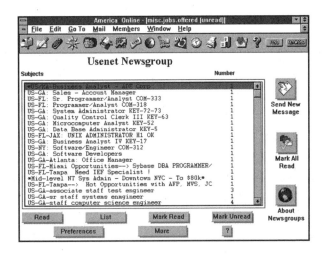

pdaxs.jobs.management
Management opportunities in Portland, Oregon.

pdaxs.jobs.retail
Retail job opportunities in Portland, Oregon.

pdaxs.jobs.sales
Sales opportunities in Portland, Oregon.

pdaxs.jobs.secretary
Secretarial job opportunities in Portland, Oregon.

sat.jobs
Employment opportunities in the San Antonio, Texas area.

sdnet.jobs
Jobs available in San Diego, California.

seattle.jobs.offered
Job opportunities in the Seattle, Washington area.

seattle.jobs.wanted
More job opportunities in Seattle, Washington.

su.jobs
Employment opportunities at Stanford University.

tx.jobs
Jobs available in Texas.

tx.wanted
More jobs available in Texas.

ucb.jobs
Employment opportunities at University of California,
    Berkeley.

vegas.jobs
Jobs available in Las Vegas, Nevada.

wyo.jobs
Employment opportunities in Wyoming.

NATIONAL
alt.medical.sales.jobs.offered
Job opportunities in medical sales.

bionet.jobs
Job opportunities in biological science.

biz.jobs.offered
Employment opportunities nationwide.

cit.jobs
Computer-related employment opportunities nationwide.

dod.jobs
Employment opportunities with the United States
     Department of Defense.

misc.jobs.offered
Job opportunities available nationwide.

misc.jobs.offered.entry
Entry-level jobs available nationwide.

prg.jobs
Computer programming job opportunities available nationwide.

sci.research.postdoc
Job opportunities in postdoctoral scientific research.

us.jobs
Jobs available in the United States.

us.jobs.contract
Contract labor and consulting opportunities in the United States.

us.jobs.misc
Employment opportunities in the United States.

us.jobs.offered
More employment opportunities in the United States.

CANADA

ab.jobs
Job opportunities in Alberta, Canada.

bc.jobs
Employment opportunities in British Columbia, Canada.

can.jobs
Jobs available in Canada.

kw.jobs
Jobs available in Kitchener-Waterloo, Canada.

nb.jobs
Jobs available in New Brunswick, Canada.

ont.jobs
Jobs available in Ontario, Canada.

ott.jobs
Job opportunities in Ottawa, Ontario, Canada.

qc.jobs
Jobs available in Quebec, Canada.

tor.jobs
Jobs available in Toronto, Ontario, Canada.

INTERNATIONAL

aus.ads.jobs
Jobs available in Australia.

bermuda.jobs.offered
Jobs available in Bermuda.

bln.jobs
Job opportunities in Berlin, Germany.

de.markt.jobs
Employment opportunities in Germany.

dk.jobs
Jobs available in Denmark.

eunet.jobs
Job opportunities in Europe.

euro.jobs
More job opportunities in Europe.

fr.jobs.offres
Employment opportunities in France.

ie.jobs
Jobs available in Ireland.

iijnet.jobs
Job opportunities in Israel.

no.marked.jobb
Employment opportunities in Norway.

swnet.jobs
Employment opportunities in Sweden.

uk.jobs
Job opportunities in the United Kingdom.

za.ads.jobs
Employment opportunities in South Africa.

THE WORLD WIDE WEB

The World Wide Web is fast becoming *the* place to look for jobs on the Internet. And with good reason. There are dozens of career resources on the Web devoted to job listings, with more springing up every day. While many contain general information regarding job hunting, a number of sites are specialized, devoting themselves to one particular field, industry, or region. Unlike Usenet newsgroups, which tend to focus on computer-related or other technical positions, the Web has listings for job hunters of all backgrounds, including those in nontraditional fields like the graphic arts and social sciences. True, those types of positions are in the minority in most job listing databases, but the point is, you don't need to be an engineer or computer programmer to take advantage of the vast career resources available online.

A Brief History of the Web

The World Wide Web came into existence in 1991, but it has really only been in the past two years that the general public has noticed and then embraced the Web. Before the Web, there was only the Internet—Usenet, Telnet, and Gopher—and then came the popularization of the non-Internet online services like Prodigy, CompuServe, and America Online. While the Internet was chiefly the territory of academics, government officials, and computer scientists, commercial online services became popular with families, due in large part to their user-friendly, graphical interfaces.

Although hypertext, the original concept behind the World Wide Web, was developed in the mid-1960s, its potential was not realized until almost thirty years later. **Hypertext allows users to access information, such as text, graphics, or music, through predetermined links.** On the Web, hypertext links are most often represented by underlined words. When a hypertext link is selected, the user is automatically transported to the linked site, which can be a completely different Web page or, as with larger sites, a file or subdirectory within the main directory. (Links may also be represented graphically, in an icon, but the results are the same as when you click on the underlined words.)

In the first few years of its existence, the Web was lightly regarded by many Internet experts, and rightly so. The Web was used almost as a new toy by computer scientists who were impressed by its graphic capabilities. Basically, the World Wide Web was interesting to look at, but offered little substantial information, so many experts dismissed the Web as a novelty that would never be a significant part of the Internet. Needless to say, they were wrong.

Many companies were quick to recognize the commercial potential of the Web. Businesses saw how the combination of graphics and text could enable them to inexpensively market their products and services to millions of potential customers, and rushed to create a home page that would allow them to do this. **Now, most major companies, as well as many smaller businesses, organizations, and associations, maintain a presence on the World Wide Web.**

This is not to say, of course, that the World Wide Web doesn't have its drawbacks. Many users complain that it's often difficult to find the exact information they're searching for; keyword searches using broad terms will often yield thousands of matching entries. For instance, a search using the word "cigar" can result in more than 40,000 matches! At the same time, boolean searches will narrow your search and result in fewer, but more precise, matches. But the biggest complaint most Web users have is how long it takes to download images from the Web. Even the fastest modem available can often take several minutes to download intricate graphic images from a host computer, which is often frustrating for users eager to dig in and find information.

However, most Web browsers allow you to turn off the graphics so that only the text of a Web document is received. If you have a slow modem, say 14.4 KBPS or lower, that's probably your best bet. At the same time, faster modems are beginning to make their way into the home market. Cable modems, which carry Internet access to your home through the same wires that bring you cable TV—and can carry up to ten *million* BPS—are being test marketed in several cities. Assuming these cable modems are a success, it will still take several years before they are the norm in most communities.

Despite its shortcomings, the Web has opened the Internet to commercial development, and put the Internet on the map for the general public. The main reason the Web is so popular is because it makes the Internet more user-friendly. Instead of typing in long lists of commands, users can simply point and click with their mouse, much like on the commercial online services that have been so popular for years. Today, the Web's user-friendliness and entertainment value remain its main attraction.

Like the web of a spider, the World Wide Web has no beginning and no end; it's a tangle of information that crosses and intersects. You can use hypertext links for hours without ever returning to the point at which you began. Almost any information is accessible through the Web; the paintings at the Musee D'Orsay in Paris (**http://www.paris.org/Musees/Orsay**); or the

latest scores and sports news on ESPN's Web page
(**http://www.espn.sportszone.com**).

URLs Demystified

Preceding the name of any Web site is a long string of seemingly
indecipherable words and letters, which is called a Uniform
Resource Locator (URL). While URLs are difficult to type in every
time you want to go somewhere on the Web (forget about trying
to memorize them), they are essential if you want to find any kind
of information on the World Wide Web. A URL is a standardized
system for finding things like files, directories, or other computers
connected to the World Wide Web. Knowing what the various letters stand for helps users remember the URLs for particular sites
and, as in the case with machine code identifiers, get a feel for
what type of information will be found there.

Every URL must have at least two parts: a protocol and a
server, or location. The protocol is simply how computers
exchange information. On the World Wide Web it's called hypertext transfer protocol, since all documents on the Web are written
using hypertext. The server is the name of the computer from
which information is received. For instance, in the URL
http://www.occ.com, the server is "occ," for the main computer
at the Online Career Center.

The United States has six basic codes to identify the type of
server:

> **.com (commercial)**
> **.edu (educational)**
> **.gov (government)**
> **.mil (military)**
> **.org (organizational)**
> **.net (network)**

A two-letter code at the end of a location name, such as the .uk in **http://www.demon.co.uk/EuroJobs**, signifies an international address. These country codes are similar to the country codes assigned in international telephone numbers.

In addition to the protocol and server, URLs will often include a directory, subdirectory, and file name. These are simply added on to the end of a URL, and are separated by single slashes. So in the URL **http://espnet.sportszone.com/nfl/news/index.html**, "espnet.sportszone.com" is the server, "nfl" is the directory, "news" is the subdirectory, and "index" is the file name.

Where to Find Job Listings on the World Wide Web

As mentioned before, the popularity of the World Wide Web is due in large part to its user-friendly, graphical interface that makes it easier to navigate than the old, text-based Internet. One of the best examples of this fact is to compare a Usenet newsgroup such as **us.jobs** with a Web site along the lines of the Monster Board (**http://www.monster.com**). A newsgroup shows only a very long list of job openings, and it's necessary to read each individual job title to get a feel for what the job is. But with the Monster Board, a job hunter can simply enter in his or her desired job category and location, and the Monster Board's search engine will find jobs that match the criteria. Thus, a few clicks of the mouse produces a personalized list of jobs for specific job hunters. (Don't, however, ignore job-related newsgroups in favor of the Web. Newsgroups contain tens of thousands of job openings that cannot be found anywhere else.)

While interesting graphics might have been what first drew job hunters to the Web, it is the veritable mountain of job-related information to be found that has kept them there. The Web has dozens of sites for job listings, and hundreds more for general job-hunting resources, such as resume banks and employer databases.

As a whole, the Web contains literally hundreds of thousands of job listings. It has government jobs, technical jobs, creative jobs, or entry-level jobs for new graduates, as well as permanent, temporary, and full- or part-time positions. You can find jobs in Australia, Japan, or in a state two time zones away, which is what makes the Web an especially attractive destination for anyone considering relocating.

The Web's job databases vary greatly in both the quality and quantity of job listings. We recommend starting with the all-purpose job hunting sites, such as CareerMosaic, E-Span, the Monster Board, and the Online Career Center. These are four of the largest and most popular job hunting sites on the Web, and they have thousands of listings for positions in all fields, in both the United States and abroad. Each also contains other helpful career resources, such as resume databases, employer profiles, and articles and tips to help you with your job hunt. Then try some of the other sites; you will probably find a favorite or two that contains the most job listings in your field. To make things easier, don't forget to bookmark those sites where you find good information and to which you would like to return.

One advantage of scanning the Web for employment opportunities is the quality of the job listings. Some job postings on the Web run as many as 500 words, a far cry from the minuscule want ad in your Sunday newspaper. These larger ads contain detailed information about the position, such as a lengthy job description and a specific list of required experience and skills.

You may also find that a number of the listings in the major job databases overlap. The same search performed on the Monster Board and CareerSite, for example, will likely retrieve many of the same listings, simply because many companies may advertise on several services at once. Be sure to keep careful records so you don't mistakenly send a resume to the same company twice for the same job listing.

In addition to the listings that follow, check out some job-related online Meta-lists, which contain additional links to thousands of other online career resources. The Career Resource Center (**http://www.careers.org**) contains thousands of links to job resources on the Web. The links are broken down into categories, like financial services, or computers and engineering. Other Meta-lists to consult include Stanford University's JobHunt (**http://www.job-hunt.org**), and Purdue University's Placement Services-Sites for Job Seekers and Employers (**http://www.purdue.edu/student/jobsites.htm**). The Riley Guide (**http://www.dbm.com/jobguide**) is another superb source of job-related resources on the Web.

Another way to find job listings on the Web is to perform a keyword search in a search engine such as Yahoo! or Magellan. Try using keywords like "employment opportunities," "job listings," or "positions available." Finally, an individual company's Web page is often an excellent source for job listings. *For more information on how to find the URLs for individual companies, see Chapter 11, Researching Companies Online.*

A brief explanation of the job listings that follow: You will find the name of the site, followed by the URL. The **Number of job listings** is rounded down; for instance, if a site had 503 job listings, we said 500; if a site had 11,128 listings, we rounded that down to 11,000. When we were unable to determine information within a reasonable degree of accuracy, N/A is used. **Types of jobs** indicates in general terms in what fields or job categories you are likely to find job listings. Similarly, **Locations of jobs** indicates for what countries, states, or cities job listings can be found. **Frequency of updates** says how often job listings are added to the database. **Search criteria available** shows you how the database can be searched. Most sites allow you to search by some combination of job category, location, company, or keywords; some let you search only by keyword. **Sponsoring companies** tells you, where available, how many companies post job listings to that site, and the names of two or three of the major companies. Like the name indicates, **Key features** discusses other career resources, besides job listings, available on the site. And **Insider tips** is our impression of a site and its resources, and other relevant information.

ACADEME THIS WEEK/ CHRONICLE OF HIGHER EDUCATION

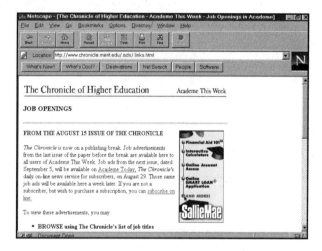

http://chronicle.merit.edu/.ads/.links.html
Number of job listings: 1,300
Types of jobs: Academic, both faculty and nonfaculty available
Locations of jobs: United States, international
Frequency of updates: Weekly
Search criteria available: Job category (and subsets within categories), keyword, and region
Sponsoring companies: Hundreds of universities and colleges, from Harvard University to University of Washington
Key features: Subscribers can see the full text of *The Chronicle of Higher Education,* the trade newspaper for academics.
Insider tips: Calling itself "the world's principal academic marketplace," this Web site contains hundreds of listings for faculty, administrative, and executive positions for prestigious U.S. colleges. The job database includes listings for related positions outside of academe, in organizations such as art galleries, government agencies, museums, and other nonprofit organizations. The site uses Gopher to access the job listings; faculty and research positions can be browsed according to subject.

AMERICA'S JOB BANK

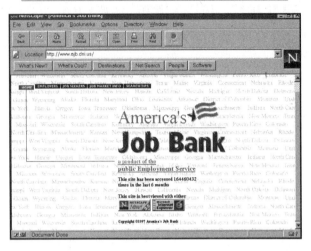

http://www.ajb.dni.us

Number of job listings: 250,000

Types of jobs: Professional, technical, blue collar, management, clerical, sales. Five percent of jobs listed are government jobs.

Locations of jobs: United States

Frequency of updates: Daily; listings less than seven days old are starred

Search criteria available: Occupation, location, keyword, or occupational code

Sponsoring companies: Names of companies not included in job listings

Key features: Contains links to the *Occupational Outlook Handbook* online, state employment service Web sites, private placement agencies, and hundreds of employer Web sites, many of which contain job listings.

Insider tips: A joint service from the United States Department of Labor and state employment offices, this is an immense database of jobs culled from the combined job databases of 1,800 state employment offices. The listings contain detailed information including a job description and educational and work requirements. Many also contain the salary range. America's Job Bank is also accessible through many public libraries, colleges, and universities. Job market trends and online tutorials are also available.

BEST JOBS USA

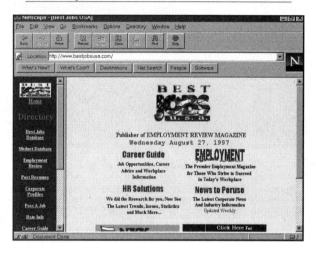

http://www.bestjobsusa.com
Number of job listings: 8,000
Types of jobs: All
Locations of jobs: United States
Frequency of updates: Daily
Search criteria available: Location, job category, and job title
or company name
Sponsoring companies: State Farm Insurance and American
Paging, among others
Key features: Best Jobs and Mednet databases, free resume
posting, and articles from the monthly publication
Employment Review online.
Insider tips: An excellent site that features both an extensive
jobs database and a smaller database focusing exclusively
on health care positions. *Employment Review* offers a wealth
of career advice to individuals and recruiting advice to
employers. There is also information about Best Jobs
Career Fairs, offered in more than 40 cities nationwide.
The site is maintained by Recourse Communications, Inc.
(RCI).

BOSTONSEARCH

http://www.bostonsearch.com

Number of job listings: 150

Types of jobs: All, but with an emphasis on technical and computer-related listings

Locations of jobs: Boston metro area

Frequency of updates: Daily

Search criteria available: Industry

Sponsoring companies: Edgewater Technology, Integrated Computer Solutions, and others

Key features: Monthly career advice column and free resume database.

Insider tips: BostonSearch is one example of a local job-hunting database, focusing exclusively on jobs and employers in the Boston metro area. The site just got up and running in the Spring of 1997, so job listings at the time of this writing were limited. However, the job database, resume database, and career services all seem to be helping this site get off to a respectable start.

CAREERBUILDER

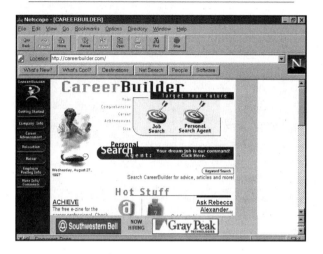

http://www.careerbuilder.com

Number of job listings: N/A

Types of jobs: All; more than 30 different categories available

Locations of jobs: United States

Frequency of updates: Daily

Search criteria available: Job category, location by state, keyword, salary range, and company name

Sponsoring companies: More than 70, including Texas Instruments and Price Waterhouse

Key features: Resume and cover letter section, career planning information and advice, a resume posting area, links to each sponsoring company's Web site, and an extensive job database.

Insider tips: CareerBuilder provides the monthly e-zine *Achieve*, which offers articles and columns about job hunting, the workplace, and starting a business. There's also a bookstore of recommended career-related books and a free personal job search agent, which allows you to use up to five search agents (so you can choose different criteria) for the same email address. CareerBuilder is maintained by NetStart, a Virginia-based software company.

CAREERCITY

http://www.careercity.com

Number of job listings: 125,000

Types of jobs: Computers, consulting, finance, health care, marketing, public relations, sales, and (noncomputer) technical

Locations of jobs: United States, some international

Frequency of updates: Daily

Search criteria available: Job category and state, or keyword search by job description, job title, and company name

Sponsoring companies: Over 2,500, including 3Com, Merck, Netpro, and People Soft

Key features: Offers a wealth of career information from best-selling job-hunting and career books; free resume posting to a large, up-to-date resume database; a search engine for 100 job-related Usenet newsgroups; and another search engine with links to over 700 companies featuring job listings on their Web sites. CareerCity also includes information on ordering career-related books and software, and a "Feature of the Day" column with career-related articles to help you with your job search.

Insider tips: CareerCity focuses on quality professional and technical job listings. The site is a service of Adams Media Corporation, the publishers of best-selling career books such as the *JobBank* series, Martin Yate's *Knock 'Em Dead*, and this book.

CAREER EXPOSURE

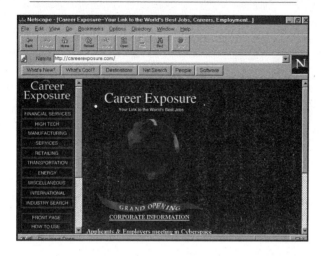

http://www.careerexposure.com

Number of job listings: N/A

Types of jobs: Financial services, high-tech, manufacturing, retailing, transportation, energy, miscellaneous

Locations of jobs: United States, some international

Frequency of updates: Daily

Search criteria available: Industry, job category, company name

Sponsoring companies: The Boeing Company, Cigna Corporation, Prudential, and many others

Key features: Thousands of job listings from major employers; links to Web sites and colleges; the e-zine "What's News" filled with career news, business happenings, and other features; and professional interviews at "Up Close and Virtual."

Insider tips: Career Exposure is essentially a compilation of job listings at large corporate Web sites, presenting those listings at their own extensive site. The quality of the listings, from a variety of well-known employers, indicates that the aim to help both employers and applicants is working. Although all types of jobs can be found here, there is definitely a focus on skilled technical workers.

CAREERMAGAZINE

http://www.careermag.com

Number of job listings: 12,000

Types of jobs: All, but emphasis on technical and computer-related listings

Locations of jobs: United States, some international

Frequency of updates: Daily

Search criteria available: Location, skills, and job title

Sponsoring companies: Thousands, from major corporations to small businesses, including 3M, Kelly Services, and EDS

Key features: Contains a resume database, employer profiles, career-related news and articles from publications such as the *National Business Employment Weekly*, and information on networking and interview preparation. The Career Forum is moderated and discusses issues concerning the job search and the workplace. Dozens of links to other employment-related sites include salary guides and an employment agency directory. An "On Campus" section is tailored toward college students, while a "Diversity" area focuses on workplace diversity and minority opportunities.

Insider tips: CareerMagazine's job database is compiled from over 100 job-related Usenet newsgroups. But CareerMagazine offers numerous other career resources to job hunters, such as the World Wide Web Resume Database and career articles. Networking opportunities include ways to post your resume directly to job fairs.

CAREERMART

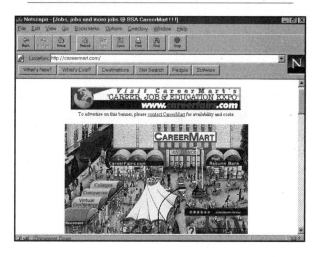

http://www.careermart.com

Number of job listings: N/A

Types of jobs: All, including engineering, accounting, clerical, and entry-level

Locations of jobs: United States, Canada, some international

Frequency of updates: N/A

Search criteria available: Location, job category, and company

Sponsoring companies: 400, including AT&T and Time-Life

Key features: E-Mail Agent, which automatically emails you when a position that matches your search criteria turns up in the database; links to the home pages of more than 400 employers; a newsstand where you can browse top publications such as *USA Today* and *Fortune*; and Career Chat, a forum for discussing career-related topics.

Insider tips: CareerMart features interesting, detailed graphics and valuable information for job hunters of all types. What is especially useful are the links to top employers across the country *and* to the Web pages of more than 700 colleges nationwide, which makes this site appealing to students and recent graduates. Also, its "ADvise" section discusses industry outlooks and projections for where the job opportunities will be in the coming years.

CAREERMOSAIC

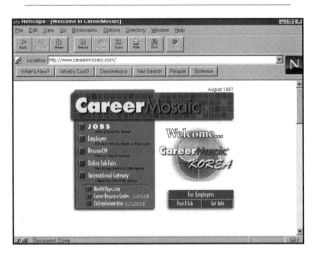

http://www.careermosaic.com

Number of job listings: 70,000

Types of jobs: All, with a focus on communications, finance, health care, high-tech, and retailing

Locations of jobs: United States, Canada, Asia, United Kingdom, France, Spain, Australia, Brazil, and more

Frequency of updates: Daily

Search criteria available: Job description and title, company, city, state, zip code, country, and keyword

Sponsoring companies: 245, including large employers such as Citibank; Deloitte & Touche, LLP; and Microsoft

Key features: Contains several international job databases, including CareerMosaic Gateway, featuring thousands of job opportunities worldwide; a searchable database of job listings from Usenet; links to hundreds of sponsoring companies; and a resume database. It also includes information for college students, such as job opportunities and programs, online job fairs, and a Career Resource Center, which gives job hunting advice as well as information on industry trends.

Insider tips: Whether you're looking for job opportunities close to home or across the globe, CareerMosaic is a must-see. It has an extensive international jobs database, but it offers more than just job listings. Job hunters of all experience levels can find advice and tips on everything from writing a cover letter to managing their career.

CAREERPATH

http://www.careerpath.com

Number of job listings: 200,000

Types of jobs: All, including accounting, advertising, executive, general office, sales, engineering, and computers

Locations of jobs: United States; newspapers from 36 major cities were represented at the time of this writing.

Frequency of updates: Weekly

Search criteria available: Newspaper name, job category, and job description keywords

Sponsoring companies: No sponsoring companies. Varies from Fortune 500 corporations to small local businesses.

Key features: Contains information on participating newspapers and the areas they cover, including links to each individual newspaper's home pages. In late 1997, CareerPath was developing an Employer Profiles section for its site, with links to each employer's home page.

Insider tips: CareerPath's job database is comprised of the Sunday employment ads from 36 major city newspapers, including the *New York Times*, *Chicago Tribune*, *Boston Globe*, *Washington Post*, *Denver Post*, *Los Angeles Times*, and *Miami Herald*. Thus, the quality of the job listings will depend on the companies that placed the ads. This is a great service for anyone considering relocating to a major city, and a great resource for researching the job market in another region.

CAREER SHOP

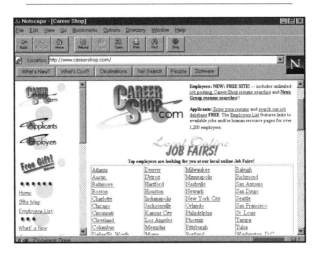

http://www.careershop.com

Number of job listings: N/A

Types of jobs: All, including professional, managerial, and technical positions

Locations of jobs: United States

Frequency of updates: Daily

Search criteria available: Company, state, and job title

Sponsoring companies: Nearly 2,000 employers have jobs posted here

Key features: Various career resources; a "preparing for the interview" section; resume posting; and an employer's list with links to nearly 2,000 employers.

Insider tips: The Employer's List features an extensive alphabetical list of companies who are currently hiring. It features not only job listings and descriptions but also links to company home pages. There are also links available to 44 online job fairs where you can post your resume.

CAREERSITE

http://www.careersite.com

Number of job listings: 3,000

Types of jobs: All, including technical, nontechnical, full- and part-time, temporary, and permanent

Locations of jobs: United States

Frequency of updates: Daily

Search criteria available: Occupation, location, and keywords for qualifications and education

Sponsoring companies: Over 250, including major corporations such as Arthur Anderson, LLP; Fidelity Investments; and Ford Motor Company.

Key features: Links to sponsoring companies give you short company profiles and job openings for specific companies. Includes SmartMatch, an interactive technology that automatically notifies you of job openings that match your credentials. Also includes a resume database.

Insider tips: CareerSite is a unique job database for job hunters. You must register in order to search the job listings. You can also fill out a "credentials" form, and submit a resume to their resume database. Once this is done, CareerSite will search the job listings for you, saving you valuable time. However, you can also register and search the database without sending in your resume or filling out a credentials form. The detailed job listings include information on job requirements and qualifications.

CAREERWEB

http://www.cweb.com

Number of job listings: 11,000

Types of jobs: All fields and experience levels, covering professional, technical, and managerial jobs

Locations of jobs: United States; some in Canada, Europe, and Japan

Frequency of updates: Weekly

Search criteria available: Job category and location, keyword, or employer

Sponsoring companies: More than 200, including such names as Foot Locker, Hewlett-Packard, and Prudential Securities

Key features: Includes employer profiles; resume registration; JobMatch, a personalized automated database search; forms for career assessments; and work values tests. Tons of career-related resources, including links to dozens of industry associations, plus tips and advice on internships and resume writing, the job hunt, and more. You can also order books, software, and videos to help you with your job search.

Insider tips: CareerWeb is packed with information and resources for job hunters. If you register your resume, you can respond to advertisements with a simple click of a button. It also has a job matching service that costs $25 for three months. Also, check out the Career Doctor for columns on finding a job, self-employment, and more.

COLLEGE GRAD JOB HUNTER

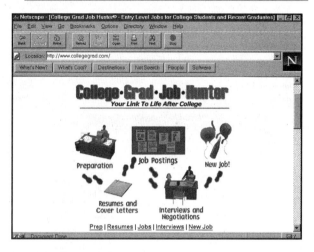

http://www.collegegrad.com

Number of job listings: N/A

Types of jobs: Entry-level and internships

Locations of jobs: United States

Frequency of updates: Daily

Search criteria available: Company, state, and job title

Sponsoring companies: More than 80 companies have jobs listed here; employer database features 3,000 employers

Key features: Job posting area, employer database, internship information, Job Hunter e-zine of career advice, and text of *College Grad Job Hunter* (Quantum Leap Publishing).

Insider tips: An attractive, well-organized site geared toward recent college graduates, offering a step-by-step guide to getting a job, everything from resume preparation to interviewing tips and negotiating an offer. Information is adapted directly from the book of the same name; the entire text of the 1997 edition is currently available online. Actual job listings are limited, but those that are available are ideal for entry-level candidates, and major employers such as Intel Corporation and Ziff-Davis Publishing detail their internship programs here. There are also links to a variety of other job hunting Web sites. This site is an excellent choice for those new to the job market.

CONTRACT EMPLOYMENT WEEKLY

http://www.ceweekly.com

Number of job listings: 3,500 for subscribers; 650 for nonsubscribers

Types of jobs: Temporary and contract technical positions

Locations of jobs: United States

Frequency of updates: Hourly

Search criteria available: Keywords and issue dates

Sponsoring companies: 500, including Avionics Research Corp. and CDI Corp.

Key features: Contains links to companies that regularly hire contract technical employees. Electronic subscriptions are available, as well as a resume service that mails your resume to employers.

Insider tips: This electronic version of *Contract Employment Weekly* has listings for thousands of short- and long-term technical positions. Unfortunately, you need to be a subscriber to access the entire database; only a portion of the database is available to nonsubscribers. However, this site should be a definite for anyone looking for technical contract work, since it boasts that the advertised positions generally pay higher than other nonpermanent work.

COOL WORKS

http://www.coolworks.com

Number of job listings: 30,000

Types of jobs: Primarily seasonal, outdoor employment at national parks, resorts, camps, and ski areas

Locations of jobs: Nationwide, but an emphasis on Western United States

Frequency of updates: Weekly

Search criteria available: Job type, location, and specific title

Sponsoring companies: College career centers and national parks, among others

Key features: Information about volunteer opportunities, links to more than 30,000 job listings, and career placement information concerning recreational employment.

Insider tips: Cool Works does a good job of covering a unique market, that of seasonal employment. Links to colleges and various large career sites enable job hunters with an interest in these kinds of jobs to get a good glimpse of what is available. Job seekers can look at opportunities at famous national parks such as Yellowstone, Mesa Verde, and Grand Teton, among others. Partnered with the Great Outdoor Recreation Pages (GORP), an organization focusing on outdoor recreation.

E-SPAN

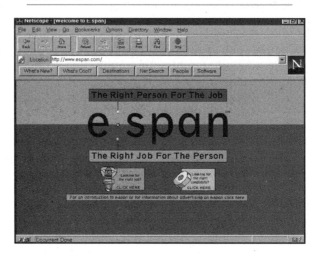

http://www.espan.com

Number of job listings: 10,000

Types of jobs: All

Locations of jobs: United States, some international

Frequency of updates: Daily

Search criteria available: Job description keywords, education and experience levels, current job level, salary requirements, and desired geographic areas

Sponsoring companies: Over 2,000, including Westinghouse and Coopers & Lybrand, LLP

Key features: Includes resume database, employer profiles with links to advertisers' home pages, job hunting tips, and articles on all facets of the job search, including resumes and interviewing. E-Span also allows Usenet searches. Finally, a reference and resource library features more than 6,000 links to career-related resources, including newspapers, career fairs, networking tips, education, and more.

Insider tips: You must register to conduct a full-blown search of the database with all your criteria. But once you register, the computer remembers all your criteria so you don't have to enter it every time. You can, of course, refine and change your personal criteria at any time. Overall, one of the best job hunting sites you can find on the Internet.

FEDWORLD FEDERAL JOB ANNOUNCEMENT SEARCH

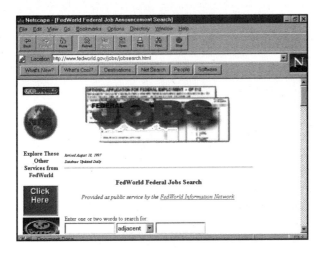

http://www.fedworld.gov/jobs/jobsearch.html
Number of job listings: 1,500
Types of jobs: All
Locations of jobs: United States, some U.S. territories
Frequency of updates: Daily, except Sunday and Monday
Search criteria available: Keywords, state, and series number (government assigned job codes)
Sponsoring companies: Departments and agencies within the federal government
Key features: Includes links to numerous other sites and access to various government databases, such as the FedWorld File Libraries, where you can find archival information on business, the environment, and many other subjects. You can also find and order information from the U.S. government.
Insider tips: This site is brought to you courtesy of the National Technical Information Services (NTIS), an agency of the U.S. Department of Commerce. The jobs database contains openings for all kinds of positions, from computer analyst to maintenance. The site is also accessible through Telnet and FTP. Fedworld has a truly impressive array of resources beyond its own job listings; you can even check out White House press releases through this site!

4WORK

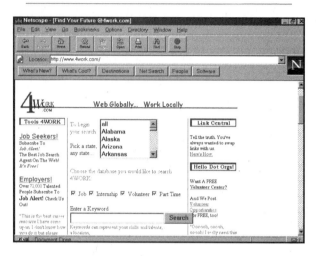

http://www.4work.com
Number of job listings: 4,000
Types of jobs: All types
Locations of jobs: United States
Frequency of updates: Daily
Search criteria available: Keyword, state, or company
Sponsoring companies: 130, including Blockbuster Video and Norrell Services
Key features: Includes job databases of volunteer positions, internships, work for high school students, and an interactive agent "Better than a Bookmark" that automatically matches job seekers with job listings. Also contains information on relocating, as well as links to numerous colleges and universities.
Insider tips: While it doesn't have the additional career resources (such as employer profiles and a resume database) offered by the Monster Board or the Online Career Center, 4WORK's jobs database is well worth the time of the search. Or better yet, if you register your personal profile—name, email address, skills—Job Alert! lets you know that an employer has posted an appropriate opportunity. This site also posts volunteer opportunities and internships, free of charge to employers.

GET A JOB

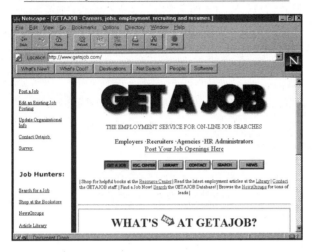

http://www.getajob.com

Number of job listings: 100

Types of jobs: All, but a focus on technical

Locations of jobs: United States, many in the San Francisco Bay area

Frequency of updates: Daily

Search criteria available: Company name, job category, and location

Sponsoring companies: 65, including Chemical Bank and Qualcomm

Key features: Newsgroup searches are available, including several international newsgroups, links to other career-related sites, and a resource center where you can purchase job resources such as books for a sizable discount. There's also a career libary with articles and columns to help your search.

Insider tips: While Get a Job's job database may not be as comprehensive as some of the other sites listed here, it is definitely worth a visit. Check out the links to other career resources, including the "In Pursuit Employment Network" and "Shawn's Internet Resume Center," which provide job hunters with links to even more sites, including resume databases and sources for job hunting tips and advice. There are even links to employment services.

HEART: CAREER CONNECTION

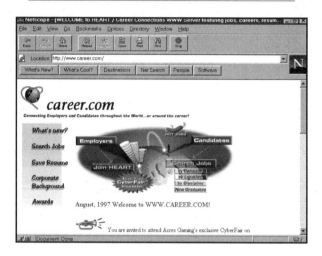

http://www.career.com

Number of job listings: 750

Types of jobs: All, including engineering, financial, marketing, technical, and sales

Locations of jobs: United States, some international

Frequency of updates: Three times a week

Search criteria available: Company, job category, location, and keyword

Sponsoring companies: 50, including Advanced Micro Devices, Inc., and Siemens Components, Inc.

Key features: Includes detailed employer profiles with links to home pages, virtual job fair, resume builder, and job database. Special search engines for entry-level and federal job listings.

Insider tips: HEART: Career Connection is a growing site that, for now, is primarily good for technical positions, although the number of positions in other areas is constantly growing. All the job listings contain the dates they were posted, making it easy for job hunters to gauge how long the listings have been floating around. The special area covering employment opportunities for new graduates is a great feature, as is the section featuring "Hot Jobs" of the week.

HELP WANTED

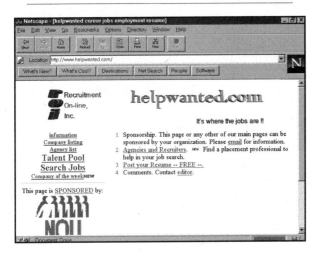

http://www.helpwanted.com

Number of job listings: N/A

Types of jobs: All, including computers, financial, technical, and management

Locations of jobs: United States, with an emphasis on the East Coast

Frequency of updates: Jobs added daily

Search criteria available: Keyword search only

Sponsoring companies: More than 150, including DRI/McGraw Hill and New England Medical Center

Key features: Includes resume database and an extensive listing of employment agencies and recruiters to help you with your job search.

Insider tips: Based on the East Coast, Help Wanted is a young and growing site for job hunters. Although its jobs database is currently on the small side, it has a wide variety of positions available. All job listings include the date on which the opening was added to the database, so you know how old the listings are. Jobs are kept in the database for no longer than two months. Run by Recruitment On-Line, Inc.

HOT JOBS

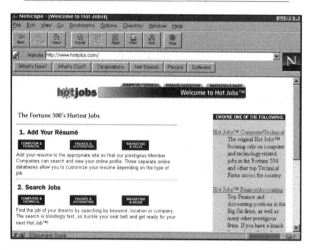

http://www.hotjobs.com

Number of job listings: 1,500

Types of jobs: Computer/technical, finance/accounting, and marketing/sales

Locations of jobs: United States, some international

Frequency of updates: Daily

Search criteria available: Keyword, location, and company name

Sponsoring companies: Best Buy, Inc., Data General, and over 140 *Fortune* 500 and high-end technical firms

Key features: Three different resume and jobs databases, a resume writing workshop, and links to company home pages.

Insider tips: In August of 1997, Hot Jobs had just added two new databases (finance/accounting and marketing/sales) to its original (computer/technical) database. Since the resume database follows suit, job seekers can customize their resumes to appropriate jobs, as well as searching in those areas that match their skills. This is a fairly straightforward jobs database that concentrates solely on jobs and companies—no recruiters or contractual firms, no career tips or features. Ideal for those who want to get right to the employment opportunities.

THE INSTITUTE OF ELECTRICAL AND ELECTRONICS ENGINEERS

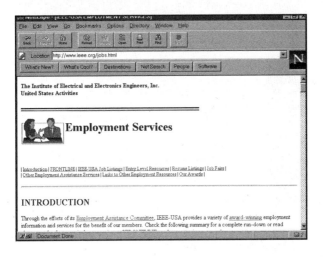

http://www.ieee.org/jobs.html

Number of job listings: N/A

Types of jobs: Electrical and technology-related jobs; entry-level engineering opportunities

Locations of jobs: United States, some international

Frequency of updates: Weekly

Search criteria available: Jobs are divided by region, including New England area, Mid-Atlantic states, non-U.S., and more

Sponsoring companies: The Institute has more than 320,000 members, including individuals and large organizations

Key features: A variety of employment services, including entry-level resources; "Resume-Link" resume posting; a schedule of technical job fairs; and regional home pages for member organizations.

Insider tips: The IEEE, the world's largest technical professional society, provides this job-listing service for electrical and electronic engineers and individuals in other related fields. Opportunities run the gamut of entry-level to experienced. Some of this site's services, like the resume posting area, require membership in the IEEE. A wealth of resources makes this site definitely worth a look for job seekers with interest and/or skills in this area.

INTELLIMATCH

http://www.intellimatch.com

Number of job listings: N/A

Types of jobs: All

Locations of jobs: United States

Frequency of updates: Daily

Search criteria available: Occupation, location, and keyword

Sponsoring companies: Analysts International Corporation, Hall Kinion, Lockheed Martin, and nearly 300 others

Key features: Jobs database; Resume Express, which allows you to create and send a text-only resume; job search agent; online career fair

Insider tips: Register your text resume and create a "Power Resume," which enables employers to match your skills to their open positions using Intellimatch's "Precision Matching" feature. A job search agent emails appropriate jobs to you quickly and easily—"finding your dream job while you sleep." The site also features success stories from other job seekers.

THE INTERNET JOB LOCATOR

http://www.joblocator.com
Number of job listings: 1,000
Types of jobs: All fields and experience levels
Locations of jobs: United States
Frequency of updates: Job listings added daily
Search criteria available: Keyword searches only
Sponsoring companies: Gateway, Volt Services Group,
 and others
Key features: Includes a resume database, which automatically
 posts resumes to the appropriate Usenet newsgroups, and
 links to other job listing sites, including the AltaVista search
 engine, Deja News, and the JobHunt Meta-list.
Insider tips: The Internet Job Locator is a simple, yet effective
 job search tool. As its name indicates, this site is strictly
 devoted to job listings. You won't see a lot of the bells and
 whistles found on other sites, but you will find more than
 1,000 job opportunities in its database. And the links to
 other job hunting sites open up thousands of more job
 possibilities. Created by Travelers OnLine.

JOBBANK USA

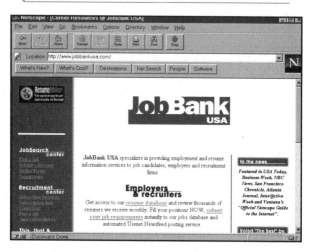

http://www.jobbankusa.com

Number of job listings: 500

Types of jobs: All, including financial, computers, public relations, and miscellaneous technical

Locations of jobs: United States

Frequency of updates: Daily

Search criteria available: Keyword, position, location, salary range, and minimum experience required

Sponsoring companies: N/A

Key features: Includes a resume database, Usenet job-related newsgroups search, and an online newspaper that features tips and job openings for international job hunters. It also has a Jobs Meta Search Page that gives you access to hundreds of thousands of jobs through other job listing services, such as E-Span.

Insider tips: The real draw of this site is its Jobs Meta Search Page. Not only can you search the JobBank USA database, but you can perform searches in the databases of several of the major World Wide Web job hunting sites, such as the Monster Board, E-Span, and the Online Career Center. Of course, if you use only this service you'll miss out on the other valuable information these services provide, but if you're short on time and only want to check out job listings, JobBank USA is an excellent choice.

JOBEXCHANGE

http://www.jobexchange.com

Number of job listings: 5,000

Types of jobs: All, including general labor and office support

Locations of jobs: South Carolina, Texas

Frequency of updates: Daily

Search criteria available: Newspaper, job title, keyword, and
date

Sponsoring companies: *The Post and Courier* in Charleston,
SC, and *The Avalanche-Journal* in Lubbock, TX

Key features: Job listings, resume posting area, links to other
sites and meta lists, and career resource center.

Insider tips: Although smaller and more focused than most of
the other Web sites presented in this chapter, JobExchange
is a good example of a site that provides newspaper
classifieds online. While obviously smaller than CareerPath,
it does offer job seekers hoping to relocate to these areas
of the country some welcome information. One note:
Listings from other newspapers, including New Jersey and
Illinois, have been included here in the past.

JOBNET

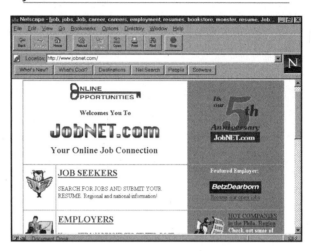

http://www.jobnet.com

Number of job listings: 500

Types of jobs: All

Locations of jobs: Philadelphia metro area

Frequency of updates: Daily

Search criteria available: Keyword, or download all jobs as a
  zip file

Sponsoring companies: Unisys, Foster Wheeler, and many
  other Philadelphia area employers

Key features: Job listings, "Online Opportunities" newsletter,
  links to partner Web sites, and information on regional job
  fairs.

Insider tips: This small, localized database is noteworthy for its
  partnerships with Web giants like the Online Career
  Center and CareerMagazine, and even moreso for its
  "Career Launcher" service that will post your resume to
  more than 400 databases, for a charge ranging from $50 to
  $75. That kind of exposure might be worth it to some, and
  indeed, the database currently boasts more than 20,000
  resumes. You can also post to JobNET's Philadelphia-area
  database for free.

JOBSERVE

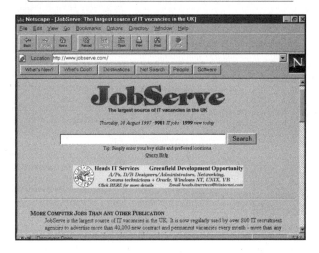

http://www.jobserve.com
Number of job listings: 40,000
Types of jobs: Information Technology, computers
Locations of jobs: The United Kingdom and throughout
    Europe; there is also a "worldwide" option
Frequency of updates: Daily
Search criteria available: Job type and region
Sponsoring companies: More than 800
Key features: Links to company Web pages, many of which
    are IT recruitment specialists; resume posting; inclusion on
    a list sent to more than 700 IT recruitment specialists
    across the UK and Europe; several different options to
    have job listings emailed to you; and a directory of
    recruiters including full contact information and email
    addresses.
Insider tips: This site helps to put the World into WWW.
    Focusing on Information Technology jobs overseas,
    JobServe has an impressive array of clever benefits for job
    seekers. "Instants" is a page on the site that features the
    newest job listings each day, and is automatically updated
    each time a position is posted online. Reload often! There
    are also options to receive the latest postings via email,
    filtered to your keyword specifications. In roughly three
    years of operation, more than 240,000 jobs have been
    advertised on this site.

JOBSOURCE

http://www.jobsource.com
Number of job listings: 500
Types of jobs: All, but mostly entry-level
Locations of jobs: United States
Frequency of updates: Daily
Search criteria available: Keyword by job title or by job category and state
Sponsoring companies: 250, including Electronic Data Systems, IBM Corp., and Market Source Corp.
Key features: Employer profiles; information on colleges and graduate schools; links to hundreds of colleges and universities; financial aid information; links to other job listing sites; a career center with related articles on interviewing and getting along after college; information on job fairs; and regional employment opportunities. Also features a resume database.
Insider tips: An excellent source of information for recent graduates, JobSource provides young job hunters with important information, presented in a fresh, light-hearted way. The vast majority of listed positions are entry-level, and there's an extensive section on internships. Also, the career articles are all written in a casual style geared for someone fresh out of college. Produced by the Monster Board (and the similarities will be obvious), JobSource truly focuses on "Careers for College Graduates."

JOBTRAK

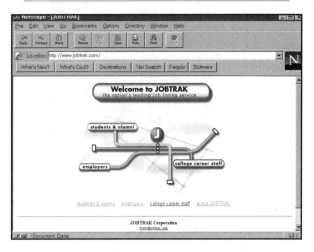

http://www.jobtrak.com
Number of job listings: N/A; 2,400 new listings each day
Types of jobs: All
Locations of jobs: United States
Frequency of updates: Daily
Search criteria available: Job type, location, keyword
Sponsoring companies: Quicken Financial Network, Sprint, and many others
Key features: Resume posting, jobs database, information from colleges and career centers, career forum, and a calendar of career fairs
Insider tips: Jobtrak's primary distinction is that its job listings are geared directly toward college students, MBA's, and alumni through college career centers. Jobtrak has formed partnerships with more than 600 college and university career centers, MBA programs, and alumni centers nationwide, to bring information from these sources to job seekers. One note: To view job listings from a particular campus, you must be a student or alumnus of that institution.

JOBWEB

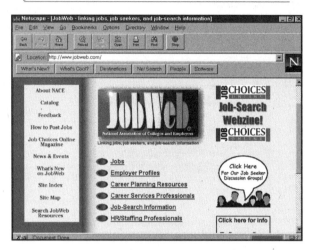

http://www.jobweb.com
Number of job listings: 3,100
Types of jobs: All fields and experience levels
Locations of jobs: United States, some international
Frequency of updates: Daily
Search criteria available: Keyword, general location; an
    advanced search lets you choose specific employment type
Sponsoring companies: 500, including Archer Daniels
    Midland Co., Merrill Lynch & Co., and SmithKline Beecham
Key features: Employer profiles and extensive listings of other
    job hunting and career resources, including links to fifty
    other job listing sites, newsgroups, and headhunters/search
    firms. Also includes information on internships and federal
    job postings, career planning resources, special
    opportunities for minorities and job hunters with
    disabilities, and a database of more than 1,200 career fairs.
    Finally, the job search and industry information section
    contains dozens of links to other business sites, like the
    Bureau of Labor Statistics and a site listing the *Fortune* 500.
Insider tips: Maintained by the nonprofit group The National
    Association of Colleges and Employers, JobWeb is truly a
    Web of useful information, with more than 100 links to
    other job hunting resources. JobWeb's employer directory
    offers detailed information, and the JobPlace discussion
    forum has more than 2,000 professional subscribers.

MBA INTERIM SOLUTIONS

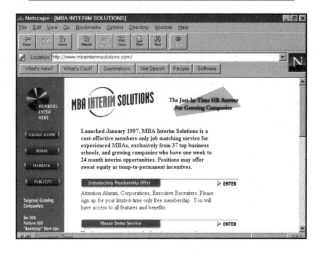

http://www.mbaintermsolutions.com

Number of job listings: N/A

Types of jobs: Interim, high-tech and business-related jobs for MBAs

Locations of jobs: United States, some international

Frequency of updates: Daily

Search criteria available: Keyword, job type, and company

Sponsoring companies: IBM, Microsoft, and many others

Key features: Job listings, email interaction between job seekers and employers/executive recruiters, and a database of alumni members.

Insider tips: Membership is required for this job matching service for experienced MBAs from top business schools. The 37 schools included (Carnegie Mellon, Harvard Business School, and many others) are all members of the International MBA placement group. According to the service, the majority of applicants meet one of the following criteria—one to fifteen years out of business school, thirty years of experience, or an independent consultant who goes from one job to the next—so clearly, this site is not for all job seekers. However, it is a good example of a job hunting Web site that focuses on a target audience and succeeds at it. Job seekers who qualify should register in the alumni members database, which is searched by employers and recruiters.

MEDSEARCH AMERICA

http://www.medsearch.com

Number of job listings: 1.200

Types of jobs: Medical/health care industry only

Locations of jobs: United States, Canada, Mexico, Europe, Asia, South America, and Africa

Frequency of updates: Daily

Search criteria available: Job category, company name, and location by city or state

Sponsoring companies: 100, including Eli Lilly & Company, Kaiser Permanente, and SmithKline Beecham

Key features: Includes a resume database (with resume builder and job search agent), employer profiles, a list of specialized recruiting agencies, and a link to the Monster Board. Job hunters can also check out the Health Care Forum, which is similar to Usenet discussion groups or the special interest groups on commercial online services. Here job hunters can post messages regarding career and other issues concerning the health care/medical industry. There's also a wealth of information on career fairs.

Insider tips: MedSearch America is one of the oldest and most respected specialized job listing sites on the Web. It contains job listings for all facets of the health care industry, everything from the business side to postings for physicians and surgeons. Anyone interested in the growing health care field should be sure to check out this site.

THE MONSTER BOARD

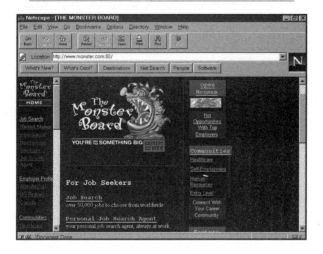

http://www.monster.com

Number of job listings: 50,000

Types of jobs: All, including technical, financial, and creative

Locations of jobs: United States, Canada, Mexico, Europe, Asia, South America, Australia

Frequency of updates: Daily

Search criteria available: Region, discipline, company and keyword—including skills, job titles, and requirements

Sponsoring companies: 1,500, including Compaq, Fidelity Investments, and IBM

Key features: Special listings for entry-level positions; a resume database; more than 4,000 employer profiles; expert job hunting and career advice; the "Monster Newsearch," which searches over forty Usenet newsgroups; a job search agent; and links to other career sites. There are also links to international sites like Monster Board UK.

Insider tips: The Monster Board is one of the best (and best known), most comprehensive job-hunting resources on the Web. It's an easy-to-use, graphically entertaining site that provides job hunters with tons of valuable information. The job listings themselves are thorough and if you have previously submitted your resume to the resume database, you can apply for positions with impressive ease. It's a true monster, too, growing all the time through partnerships with other job-hunting sites.

NATIONJOB NETWORK

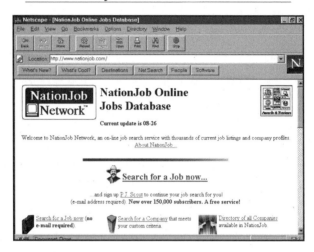

http://www.nationjob.com

Number of job listings: N/A

Types of jobs: All, including business, education, childcare, engineering, legal, and government

Locations of jobs: United States, some international

Frequency of updates: Daily

Search criteria available: Field, location, education level, keyword, and company name

Sponsoring companies: More than 700, including Ameritech and Prudential

Key features: Extensive jobs database, a job search agent, a variety of specialty Web pages, and links to Web sites of many sponsoring companies (all of whom have current job openings posted).

Insider tips: NationJob Network is a network of recruitment services presented by NationJob, Inc., which has been providing computerized job listings since 1988. They promote job openings through both Gopher and the World Wide Web, and maintain a network of stand-alone computers in many libraries, outplacement centers, military bases, and other public areas. Check out P.J. Scout, a job search agent that emails job seekers about available positions. Also, specialty pages enable job seekers to research companies in a particular employment category or geographical area. Definitely worth a look.

THE ONLINE CAREER CENTER

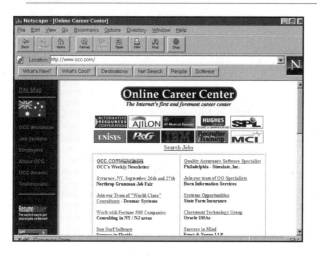

http://www.occ.com

Number of job listings: 30,000

Types of jobs: All, including banking/financial, medical/health care, computer-related, and manufacturing

Locations of jobs: United States and international, including Canada, Europe, and Mexico

Frequency of updates: Daily

Search criteria available: Keyword, industry, state, city, company, and type of employment

Sponsoring companies: 750 member companies, including AT&T, IBM, and MCI.

Key features: Includes a resume database and information on employment agencies and search firms, career fairs, and career resources for women and minorities. Career Assistance has links to other job hunting sites on the Web.

Insider tips: The original online resource for job hunters, the Online Career Center is still among the best Web sites available for job hunters. The thousands of available job listings contain detailed information on the position and its requirements, and include the date posted so job seekers know how long the job's been available. But the OCC's employer profiles and general job hunting information alone make the site worth a visit. Also, searches by state offer links to major newspapers, apartment guides, maps, costs of living, telephone directories, and more!

PASSPORT ACCESS

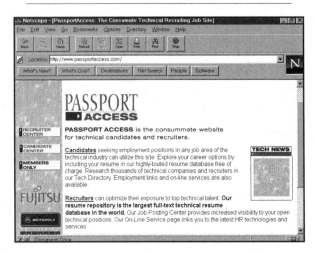

http://www.passportaccess.com

Number of job listings: N/A

Types of jobs: Technical

Locations of jobs: United States

Frequency of updates: Daily

Search criteria available: Keyword, job type, and location by state and area code

Sponsoring companies: Fujitsu, Motorola, and many others

Key features: An extensive database of job listings, a resume database, and a special Hot Jobs section (organized by company) with new positions posted daily.

Insider tips: Focusing on technical candidates and recruiters, Passport Access enables you to see a company's entire list of available postings, go to the company's Web site, or see what the position's requirements are before visiting it. Also, be sure to check out the Candidate Services page, which features direct links to computer magazines (*Byte*, *PC World*), shareware sites (Jumbo), career and resume services, electronic resume information, online books, and much, much more. Definitely worth the trip.

RETAIL JOBNET

http://www.retailjobnet.com

Number of job listings: N/A

Types of jobs: Advertising, public relations, buying, field management, and human resources

Locations of jobs: United States

Frequency of updates: Weekly

Search criteria available: National region, state, metro area, job category, and position title

Sponsoring companies: Retail Search Consultants, Inc. and Barnes & Associates Retail Search

Key features: Resume posting (for a fee); job listings

Insider tips: A small and relatively new site, Retail JobNet is noteworthy in part for its message— "Recruiting on the Internet is now a recruiting tool for everyone, not just the 'technical' people." Indeed; more industry specific sites like this, and the aforementioned MedSearch America, will no doubt be cropping up over the next several years. This site is focused exclusively on positions for professionals in the retail industry, and is working diligently to add listings and sponsors; thus the small ($15 for three months, $25 for six months) fee for its resume database.

TOPJOBS

http://www.topjobsusa.com

Number of job listings: 50,000

Types of jobs: All, including professional, managerial, and technical positions

Locations of jobs: Emphasis on Western United States—Arizona, California, Colorado, Nevada, New Mexico, Texas, and Utah—but jobs available nationwide

Frequency of updates: Twice weekly; listings purged every thirty days

Search criteria available: Company, state, and job title

Sponsoring companies: The employer database offers information on more than 60,000 employers

Key features: An immense area for employer profiles (still under construction) and a directory of recruiters and employment agencies. Offers links to other career resources, including classifieds and general job listing sites.

Insider tips: This comprehensive site has received plenty of critical praise, and for good reason. While touted as a service for the Western United States, TOPJobs contains thousands of job listings for the Midwest and the East. Most of the positions are fairly high-level, and many job listings are blind, which means that they do not contain the company name, only the address. Also, check out Career Central, offering career and networking tips. Coming soon is an area geared specifically toward college graduates.

USA JOBS

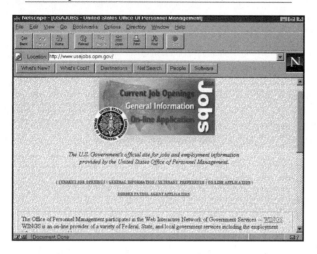

http://www.usajobs.opm.gov/

Number of job listings: N/A

Types of jobs: All, including professional, clerical, technical, and summer work

Locations of jobs: United States

Frequency of updates: Daily

Search criteria available: Job category, job title, geographic area, and salary

Sponsoring companies: N/A

Key features: Extensive job database, online career transition assistance provided by the United States Department of Labor, and various government information sources.

Insider tips: Run by the United States Office of Personnel Management, USA Jobs is the U.S. government's official site for jobs and employment information. It contains information on: applying for federal jobs, the Presidential Management Intern Program, student employment, and more. Jobs are neatly divided into professional, clerical and technical; trades and labor; senior executive; entry-level; and summer positions. You can also conduct an alphabetical search of available jobs.

VIRTUAL JOB FAIR

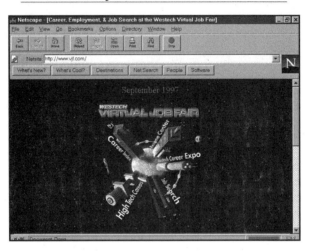

http://www.vjf.com
Number of job listings: 15,000
Types of jobs: All, with a focus on high-tech
Locations of jobs: United States, some international
Frequency of updates: Daily
Search criteria available: Keyword, company, and location by
    city and state
Sponsoring companies: More than 500, including Fujitsu and
    Space Systems/Loral
Key features: Jobs database; resume center; career index
    including the publication *High Technology Careers*; a library
    of resources, where you can search books, newsgroup
    databases, and other high-tech databases; and the Westech
    career expo, with dates and locations available for career
    fairs nationwide.
Insider tips: Virtual Job Fair is an extensive site with much to
    recommend it, particularly its Library of Career Resources.
    There is a wealth of information for job seekers here,
    including links to hundreds of articles offering career
    advice, other high-tech databases, academic and college
    employment databases, daily newspapers, and even a
    selection of international job hunting sites. Produced by
    Westech.

YAHOO!

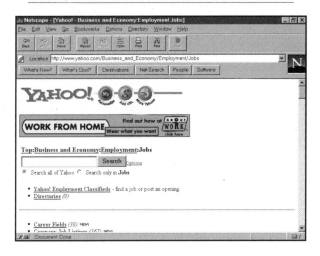

**http://www.yahoo.com/Business_and_Economy/
Employment/Jobs**
Number of job listings: N/A
Types of jobs: All
Locations of jobs: United States
Frequency of updates: Daily
Search criteria available: Keyword, location, and job function
Sponsoring companies: N/A
Key features: Job listings, section focusing on different career
   fields, job fairs, information on seasonal and summer
   employment, and Usenet sources.
Insider tips: Yahoo! is perhaps best known for its Web
   searching capabilities, and its regionalized information for
   cities and states is especially impressive. Also impressive
   are its job search capabilities, as the listings that can be
   found through Yahoo! rival those of the best job-hunting
   Web sites. Those familiar with Yahoo! know you can begin
   your search by state and often by city; for example, Boston
   residents will want to check out Yahoo! Boston. One area
   job seekers will benefit from is Yahoo! Classifieds, which
   features many thousands of employment ads in all fields,
   broken down by metro region. You can also search
   nationally or by company name.

CHAPTER SEVEN

GOPHER
AND
TELNET

So far, we have recommended using commercial online services, newsgroups, and the World Wide Web to find job listings. Now, we will examine the last two pieces of the Internet puzzle, Gopher and Telnet, which have long been favorites of job hunting experts because of the excellent employment resources found there. Today, however, many services are closing their Gopher and Telnet sites in favor of the World Wide Web. But while they may not contain the large number of general job resources now found on the Web, or in newsgroups, Gopher and Telnet remain excellent sources for specialized, high-quality job listings.

Gopher

Before the Web, there was Gopher. Named after the mascot at the University of Minnesota—where it was developed—**Gopher is often called the "grandparent technology" to the World Wide Web.** Gopher organizes its information into easy-to-use menus, which make navigating Gopherspace virtually effortless. Simply click on a menu choice, which, like on the Web, is represented by underlined words, and you will be instantly (or slowly, depending on your modem speed), transported to that server. Unlike the Web, however, Gopher does *not* use hypertext links or graphics to convey information.

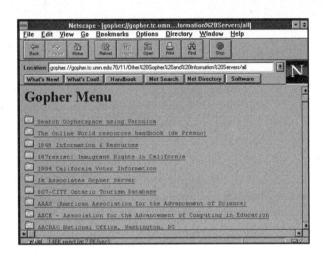

Users may connect to a Gopher server in four different ways: directly through their Internet provider, through Telnet, through their Web browser, or through a commercial online service. America Online in particular has an excellent Gopher connection, complete with a list of "Gopher Treasures" (keyword: **gopher**), a directory of the most interesting and informative sites available through Gopher.

Like the Web, Gopher contains thousands of sites providing a wide variety of information. For instance, you may search the Timeline of Counterculture, or tune in to discover the latest political happenings at C-Span's Gopher server. Lists of all Gopher servers are found in three main directories (click on the "Gopher Directory' icon in AOL's Gopher site). Gopher Jewels (**Gopher://cwis.usc.edu/11/**) organizes its list into subjects, as does Rice University's Gopher Directory (**Gopher://riceinfo.rice.edu**). Finally, All the Gopher Servers in the World (**Gopher://Gopher.tc.umn.edu**), the root Gopher server at the University of Minnesota, is a list of every Gopher site available throughout the world, organized alphabetically or by continent. At the same time, it's easy to search through these vast directories with the help of the Gopher search engines Veronica and Jughead. Veronica is the bigger of the two, but both allow users to perform a keyword search in order to locate specific information, such as Gopher sites with job listings.

Since the advent of the World Wide Web, however, growth of the Gopherspace has come to a virtual standstill. Few new Gopher sites are being created, and many are shutting down and reappearing as sites on the World Wide Web. Additionally, services that have been maintaining both a Gopher and Web presence, such as the Online Career Center, are shutting down their Gopher servers in growing numbers.

But today, Gopher is still a viable source for job listings. Although you will not find the large, all-purpose job databases containing 100,000 job listings like those found on the Web, you will find thousands of job listings in a number of fields, particularly academia. In addition to the two academic sites listed in this chapter, Academic Physician and Scientist and Academic Position Network, more than thirty colleges and universities post their job listings through Gopher, a reflection of the academic roots of the service. Users will also find job openings at the Library of Congress, and for such highly specialized jobs as economists and medical therapists. In fact, Gopher is one area where job hunters in traditional fields, such as computers, engineering, or finance, are likely to come up empty.

In the listings that follow, you will find the name of the site, followed by its address. The **Number of job listings** is rounded down; for instance, if a site had 503 job listings, we said 500; if a site had 11,128 listings, we rounded that down to 11,000. When we were unable to determine information with a reasonable degree of accuracy, N/A is used. **Types of jobs** indicates in general terms what fields or job categories you are likely to find job listings for; similarly, **Locations of jobs** indicates for what countries, states, or cities job listings can be found. **Frequency of updates** indicates how often job listings are added to the database. **Search criteria available** shows you how the database can be searched by job category, location, company, or keywords. **Key features** discusses other career resources, besides job listings, available on the site. And **Insider tips** gives our impression of a given site and its resources.

ACADEMIC PHYSICIAN AND SCIENTIST

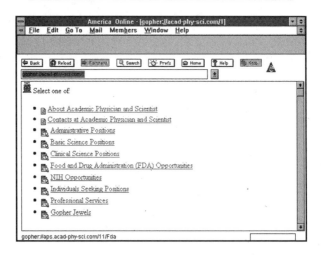

Gopher://aps.acad-phy-sci.com/

Number of job listings: 500

Types of jobs: Administrative, basic science, and clinical positions in academic medicine

Locations of jobs: United States

Frequency of updates: Daily

Search criteria available: Category and specialty; basic science and clinical databases searchable by specialty, location, or keyword

Key features: Also includes some employment opportunities with the Food and Drug Administration and the National Institute of Health. There's also an area to post situations wanted messages.

Insider tips: Academic Physician and Scientist is *the* place to find positions at teaching hospitals throughout the country. The site includes positions for chiefs of staff, assistant professors, professors, and department heads. Listings cover all fields and specialties, though the greatest number of job listings are for clinical positions.

ACADEMIC POSITION NETWORK

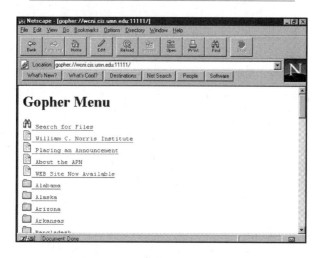

Gopher://wcni.cis.umn.edu:11111
Number of job listings: 100
Types of jobs: Faculty and administrative positions at colleges and universities
Locations of jobs: United States and international
Frequency of updates: Daily
Search criteria available: State
Key features: Includes some information on fellowships and grants
Insider tips: This is an excellent source of job listings for those interested in pursuing a career in academia. You can find employment opportunities in all fields of interest, including the humanities, social sciences, natural sciences, and more, as well as listings for deans, assistant professors, and professors. Academic Position Network also has a new Web page at **http://www.umn.edu/apn.**

ARTJOB

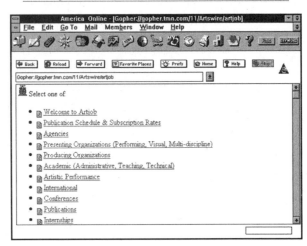

Gopher://gopher.tmn.com/11/Artswire/artjob

Number of job listings: 45

Types of jobs: Positions in the arts, including theater, dance, opera, and museums

Locations of jobs: United States, some international

Frequency of updates: Biweekly

Search criteria available: Category

Key features: Includes information on internships, grants, competitions, and conferences

Insider tips: A service of the Western States Arts Federation, ArtJob is a rarity on the Internet—a site devoted to job listings in the arts. The positions are divided into three categories: presenting organizations, producing organizations, and artistic performance. The jobs cover a wide spectrum of the arts—from a museum director in Sundance, Wyoming to an Elvis impersonator in Long Island.

Telnet

Along with Gopher and Usenet, Telnet is one of the oldest and smallest areas of the Internet. It is also unique because it is both a type of Internet site and a way to connect to a site. For instance, you may either directly connect to a Telnet site, or you may Telnet to a different type of site, such as Gopher. Telnet is very similar to the Bulletin Board Systems discussed in Chapter 8 in that it enables users to directly connect to another computer. The difference is that Telnet sites are attached to the Internet, not just a modem.

Like Bulletin Board Systems, Telnet sites are easily accessible; all you need to do is type in the address at a Telnet prompt. Most Internet service providers offer users a direct Telnet connection, but many Web browsers also provide Telnet access. (If you are using a Web browser to access Telnet, you simply need to type in "Telnet://" before the regular address.) Some commercial online services offer a direct Telnet connection; with others, you may use their Web browser for access.

Telnet was once one of the best places to look for job listings and other information online. For instance, many libraries once kept their entire card catalogs available through Telnet; now, those same card catalogs can be found on the Web. In fact, **even more rapidly than Gopher, many Telnet sites are shutting down their Telnet connection and designing new Web sites**; at the time of this writing, we were able to locate only two working Telnet sites with job listings. However, they are both extremely useful sites and well worth a visit. And, just to show there is always an exception to the rule, one of the sites listed here, H.E.A.R.T.'s Career Connection, maintains strong sites on both Telnet *and* the World Wide Web.

When you visit these sites, you will be asked to register with the service, much like a BBS. Then, you will be asked to choose a password, which you must use to access the sites in future visits.

FEDERAL JOB
OPPORTUNITIES BOARD

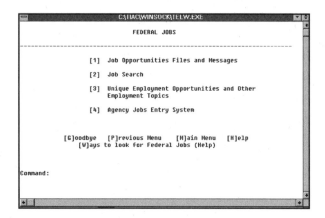

fjob.opm.gov
Number of job listings: 3,800
Types of jobs: Positions available with the U.S. government
Locations of jobs: United States and its territories
Frequency of updates: Daily
Search criteria available: Job series and titles, department or
　　agency, and state
Key features: Application information and instructions, general
　　schedule pay plan, resume templates in ASCII, and
　　recruitment bulletins. Also includes areas with job
　　opportunities overseas and opportunities for people with
　　disabilities. Also contains an area for leaving public
　　messages, such as situations wanted postings
Insider tips: This is a must-see for job hunters interested in
　　working for the federal government. Here you can
　　discover all there is to know about getting a job with the
　　U.S. government, including a step-by-step explanation of
　　the application process. Additionally, all federal job files are
　　also available for downloading, which means you can save
　　money by browsing job listings and other information
　　offline.

H.E.A.R.T.'S CAREER CONNECTION

career.com

Number of job listings: 1,000

Types of jobs: All, including technical, professional, and administrative

Locations of jobs: United States, some international

Frequency of updates: Three times a week

Search criteria available: Job category

Key features: Employer profiles, virtual job fair, resume builder, and database for posting resumes. Special sections for entry-level and federal job listings

Insider tips: This is the original Telnet version of the popular Web site. It contains all the same valuable information as the Web site, except without the graphics. Consequently, it may be wise for users with slow modems to use this version instead of waiting for the elaborate graphics to be loaded in the Web version.

CHAPTER EIGHT

BULLETIN BOARD SYSTEMS

Bulletin Board Systems are an often overlooked online resource for job listings. These days, it seems everyone is more interested in the World Wide Web and services like the Online Career Center or CareerMosaic. But job-related bulletin boards can contain up to 10,000 job listings! And Bulletin Board Systems, or BBSs as they are often called, are much easier to connect to than the World Wide Web. To connect to a BBS, all you need is a computer, a modem, and a telephone line.

Bulletin Board Systems have been around since 1978. Basically, a BBS is a computer set up with special software that you access by using a regular telephone line and the communications software on your computer. They were created as a way for people to exchange information and discuss ideas, much like a Usenet newsgroup.

The bad news is that as the World Wide Web has continued to grow in popularity, BBSs are dropping like flies. Even *Boardwatch* magazine, which once called itself "The Official Guide to Bulletin Board Systems," now goes by a broader subtitle, "The Guide to Internet Access, BBS, and the World Wide Web."

That said, BBSs remain excellent sources of information, services, and entertainment. You can find thousands of files available for downloading, including new freeware and shareware; you can participate in multi-user games; or you can simply chat with other users about various topics of interest.

The most frequent complaint against bulletin board systems continues to be the difficulty in finding out what Bulletin Board Systems exist in a particular area. If you have access to the World Wide Web, try a search engine like Yahoo! or a commercial online service like America Online to find bulletin boards in your area. Check out The BBS Corner (keyword: **BBS**) on AOL; it's also available on the Web (**http://www.thedirectory.org.**).

Besides job listings, employment-related BBSs may contain a resume database and online discussion area, and provide users with access to the Internet and Usenet newsgroups. And job hunters interested in finding technical positions, or jobs in federal, state, or local governments, should take special notice of the number of BBSs dedicated to those areas.

The below listings represent the extent of the employment-related BBSs we could unearth during production of this book. It is worth mentioning that more than half of the sites covered in the 1997 edition were no longer in service just one year later, and have been deleted accordingly. The most reliable sites are maintained by the federal government, and those are also available on the World Wide Web. It seems fair to say that BBSs of job listings are quickly becoming a thing of the past. That said, in the interest of being thorough, those whose existence we could verify have been included.

After connecting to a new BBS, you will be required to register in order to use any of the services provided. This is done to protect the service and discourage casual users from tying up the phone lines. Since most BBSs have only a limited number of phone lines (some may have only four or five), the system operators, or sysops, also limit the number of minutes users can spend on the system in one day. For example, the systems listed here allowed a maximum of one hour of use per day.

One note: Remember that while these services are free, you will be charged the cost of a regular long-distance telephone call while you are connected to the BBS. For this reason, try calling during off-hours to minimize your phone bill.

Exec-PC
414-789-4210
This is an enormous BBS with thousands of files available for download, including job listings nationwide. Also contains local access numbers for users dialing long-distance.

Federal Job Opportunities Board (FJOB)
912-757-3100
Sponsored by the U.S. Office of Personnel Management, this BBS contains federal job listings and other employment information.

ISCA (Information Systems Consultants Association) BBS
770-491-1335
Includes jobs listings, a resume database, and an online conference area where experienced information system consultants exchange ideas and information.

MacEAST
617-899-0020
National listings for technical positions. Also includes a resume database, online discussion area, and access to employment-related newsgroups.

OPM Mainstreet
202-606-4800
Includes federal job listings from the Office of Personnel Management, as well as access to other federal job BBSs and employment-related mailing lists and Usenet newsgroups.

Online Opportunities
610-873-7170
Job listings for the Philadelphia, Pennsylvania area, as well as national listings from Help Wanted USA and E-Span. Also contains a resume database, employment hotlines directory, and other online career resources.

Traders Connection
317-359-5199
This comprehensive BBS contains the classifieds from a variety of publications nationwide. Also includes a search agent which automatically searches the database for ads that meet a specified criteria.

CHAPTER NINE

COMPANY JOBLINES

The technology of the touch-tone telephone has brought a number of conveniences to our daily life. Just think of it: Without the touch-tone telephone, how would you be able to check your home answering machine to see if anyone called you for a job interview? What's more, one simple phone call now enables you to check your bank account balance, pay a parking ticket, buy tickets for a movie, renew your car registration, and—most importantly—look for a job!

Joblines, or job hotlines as they are also called, are one of the best-kept secrets of job hunting. Recorded joblines, maintained by private companies, government agencies, colleges, or industry associations, typically contain current job openings for all types of positions in industries like health care, retail, hospitality, and manufacturing. Joblines offer clerical or blue-collar positions, as well as listings for professional and middle-management openings.

When you call most joblines, a voice reads off a list of all available job openings within that company. Some include a menu of different fields—such as administrative, financial, or public relations—so you only have to listen to those job openings of interest to you. In either case, a jobline announcement typically includes a brief description of the position, along with a list of the required or recommended skills for each position. It may also give a salary range for the position, as well as information on hours or company benefits.

Joblines also include instructions on how to apply for a particular position, or with the company in general. These recorded announcements give the company address, fax number, or email address where you can send your resume or pick up an application for employment. Most joblines give you a job code that corresponds with each listed position, and you must write this job code somewhere on your application to indicate which job you're applying for. It is important to listen to these instructions carefully, since many companies toss out resumes or applications if they don't meet the specific job requirements, or stop taking applications or resumes for a position after a specified period of time.

Most companies update their joblines weekly and mention which day on the jobline. The openings announced on the joblines are often the only source of advertising for the positions, so it's important to check the joblines regularly—usually the evening or morning after they are updated is best.

One of the biggest advantages of joblines is their convenience. **Most joblines are operated seven days a week, twenty-four hours a day.** This allows you to call companies from your own home, so you won't need to worry about your boss or colleagues discovering your job search. Joblines are also useful if you want to work for one particular company. You can check in regularly for suitable openings, without worrying about being branded a pest by the human resources department.

Naturally, you shouldn't use joblines—or any single job hunting method—as your only source of job leads. While joblines can provide you with a number of previously hidden job opportunities, you should continue to explore every method and technology available.

The listings that follow represent only a small sampling of the joblines available nationwide. These 25 numbers from well-known companies will give you an idea of what recorded joblines have to offer, and help get you started. For a much larger and more diverse list of joblines, consult such books as *The National Job Line Directory* (Robert Schmidt, Adams Media Corporation) or *The National Job Hotline Directory* (Marcia P. Williams and Sue A. Cubbage, McGraw-Hill). You can also phone large companies you are interested in working for to find out if a jobline is available. Note that while most phone numbers listed are direct lines to a recorded message, with some numbers you must actually punch in an extension or ask the receptionist in order to be connected to the jobline. Also, while we have tried to ensure the accuracy of the information listed here, there can be no guarantee of its currency by the time this book reaches stores.

ALASKA

Anchorage Daily News
Anchorage
907-257-4402
Publishing (newspapers)

ARIZONA

Safeway Stores Inc.
Phoenix
602-894-4138
Retail (grocery stores, manufacturing, and distribution facilities)

CALIFORNIA

CBS Television Network
Los Angeles
213-852-2008
Communications (television broadcasting)

Citicorp/Citibank
San Francisco
415-658-4JOB
Banking

KPMG Peat Marwick LLP
San Francisco
415-951-7821
Accounting/management consulting

Charles Schwab & Company
San Francisco
415-627-7227
Financial services

University of California, Irvine
Irvine
714-UCI-JOBS
Four-year public university

COLORADO

US WEST Communications
Englewood
303-896-7683
Telecommunications

DELAWARE

First USA
Wilmington
302-594-8050
Banking

DISTRICT OF COLUMBIA

Arthur Andersen LLP
Washington, DC
202-862-8001
Accounting/management consulting

**National Education
Association (NEA)**
Washington, DC
202-822-7642
Education

GEORGIA

National Data Corporation
Atlanta
404-728-2030
*Computers (information systems
and services)*

IDAHO

Hewlett Packard Company
Boise
208-396-5200
*Computers (printers, storage, and
disk drives)*

Micron Technology
Boise
208-368-4141
*Electronics (manufactures
semiconductors)*

ILLINOIS

Federal Express Corporation
Chicago
773-601-2178
Transportation (freight delivery)

INDIANA

Eli Lilly & Co.
Clinton
800-892-9121
*Pharmaceuticals (research and
development)*

Purdue University
West Lafayette
765-494-7417
Four-year public university

MASSACHUSETTS

Ziff-Davis Publishing Company
Medford
617-393-3032
Publishing

NEW YORK

Eastman Kodak Company
Rochester
716-724-4609
*Manufacturer (photographic
equipment and supplies)*

RHODE ISLAND

Brown University
Providence
401-863-9675
Four-year private university

SOUTH DAKOTA

Gateway 2000
North Sioux City
605-232-2222
Computers (manufacturer)

VERMONT

Ben & Jerry's Homemade Inc.
Waterbury
802-651-9600, x7584
Food (ice cream products)

VIRGINIA

Allstate Insurance Company
Fairfax
800-999-6693
Insurance

WASHINGTON

The Boeing Company
Seattle
206-544-3111
Aerospace

WISCONSIN

OshKosh B' Gosh Inc.
Oshkosh
414-232-4410
Manufacturing (children's clothing)

PART THREE

TAPPING THE HIDDEN JOB MARKET

CHAPTER TEN

ELECTRONIC
EMPLOYER
DATABASES

Researching potential employers used to be one of the most time-consuming tasks of the job hunt. You would need to spend hours checking reference books, trade journals, and newspapers simply to find information on one particular company. And that was only to put together a list of potential employers to target in your job search! Once you actually scheduled an interview, you were in for even more work. Since most job hunting experts recommend arriving at an interview knowing a company inside and out, you had to go back to those same sources and find out even *more* information about a particular company. It's enough to wear out even the most dedicated job hunter.

Imagine if all this information was accessible through just a few keystrokes on a computer. Sound too good to be true? Well, with the help of **electronic employer databases** and **business periodical databases**, it's possible. These directories, which are generally available on CD-ROM, can contain detailed information on up to *ten million* U.S. and international companies. (*Online databases are discussed in Chapter 11.*) Other databases include news articles from business and trade publications, or press releases and other material from individual companies. What all this means to the job hunter is that you no longer have to spend hours in the library, searching through three different 2,000-page reference books just to find out the names of twenty companies in your city that are likely to hire someone like you. You no longer need to go through dozens of old periodicals and newspapers simply to find two or three relevant articles about the company you're interviewing with next week. With electronic employer and business periodical databases, that same information is available in just minutes.

Creating Your Target List of Companies

Advance research is essential in any job hunt. Otherwise, you could waste time sending resumes to companies that haven't hired for your position in years, or that don't have the type of atmosphere you're looking for (in terms of company size, for example). One of the first steps in any job hunt is deciding what companies are likely to hire someone with your skills and experience and, of those companies, which ones would you like to work for. The easiest way to do this is to first sit down and think about what you want to do, and in what type of atmosphere you'd like to do it.

Decide what type of company you want to work for. Look at geographical location, product line, company size, and customer type (such as industrial or consumer). Try to figure out at which companies your skills can be best put to use, and what are the most commonly hired positions at these companies. Once you have developed a list of desired criteria, you can use **electronic employer databases** to come up with a list of potential employers.

While most company directories are not specifically designed for job hunting, they contain a tremendous amount of valuable information for anyone looking for another job. Most directories will give you the same basic information, such as company name, description, address, phone and fax numbers, and number of employees. Virtually all directories will list one or more contacts, so you know exactly whom to call for information or where to send your resume. Others will also give you the name of the parent company or subsidiaries, email or home page address, product information, biographical information on key personnel, and financial information. Some directories are broad and include companies of all sizes and industries, while others are specialized according to industry, size, or company revenue.

Electronic employer databases offer a wide variety of search options. Standard & Poor's Register alone has fifty-five different search possibilities. The most basic are by geographic location or industry, so you can look for all the companies in your field that are located in your city or state. Other common search options are company size or revenue, SIC code (which stands for Standardized Industrial Code), or zip code. Some databases can be searched by job title, parent company name, stock symbol, or where key personnel went to undergraduate or graduate school. In the Martindale-Hubbell Law Directory, for instance, you could search for the names of all attorneys born in 1950 who went to Harvard Law School.

Employer databases can be especially helpful to job seekers considering relocation. You can find out, before you move, if you will realistically be able to find work once you get there. You can search for companies in virtually any region of the country, and you can get a head start on your job hunt by sending out resumes and cover letters before you move. Another big advantage of electronic employer databases is their timeliness. Most printed directories are only updated once a year, and simply because of the nature of print publishing, you could be looking at information that is even older. Most electronic database publishers, in contrast, release new versions of their databases more than once a year. Many even update their information monthly or quarterly, which means that you will always find up-to-date information concerning a company's address, phone number, key personnel, and financial condition.

One word of caution: Before using an employer database, you should have a pretty clear picture of the type of company you want to work for. While employer databases can be great tools for job hunters, they're virtually worthless if you have no idea what you want to do.

Since most of these databases cost upwards of $500 and are designed for use by other businesses or libraries, don't expect to find these at your local software store. Of course, not all libraries will have all of these resources. Depending on how technologically advanced your library is, you may only find one or two of these electronic databases. Call your library to find out what electronic resources it has available. Many of these databases can also be found in the offices of career counselors or outplacement specialists, and are used as part of your service.

Employer Databases

Adams JobBank FastResume Suite
260 Center Street, Holbrook, MA 02343
800-USA-JOBS
Produced by Adams Media Corporation, this CD-ROM creates professional-quality resumes in minutes. Another of its primary features, however, is a database of more than 22,000 companies searchable by state, industry, and/or position. Adams JobBank FastResume Suite is compatible with Windows 3.1 and Windows 95, and can be found at most stores carrying software or direct from Adams Media.

American Big Business Directory
5711 South 86th Circle, P.O. Box 37347, Omaha, NE 68127
800-555-5211
American Big Business Directory has profiles of 160,000 privately and publicly held companies with over 100 employees. The CD-ROM contains company descriptions which include type of company, industry, products, and sales information. This database also includes multiple contact names for each company, more than 340,000 in all. You can search the database by industry, SIC Code, sales volume, employee size, or zip code. The database also allows you to conduct searches of private or public companies. American Big Business can be found in many public or college libraries.

American Manufacturer's Directory

5711 South 86th Circle, P.O. Box 37347, Omaha, NE 68127
800-555-5211

Made by the same company that created American Big Business Directory, American Manufacturer's Directory lists over 531,000 manufacturing companies of all sizes and industries. The directory contains product and sales information, company size, and a key contact name for each company. The CD-ROM can be searched by region, SIC code, sales volume, employee size, or zip code. American Manufacturer's Directory is available at most college and university libraries.

Business America on CD-ROM

5711 South 86th Circle, P.O. Box 27347, Omaha, NE 68127
800-555-5211

Also from the makers of the American Big Business Directory and American Manufacturer's Directory, this CD-ROM is the most extensive, containing information on more than ten million U.S. companies. The profiles give you contact information, including contact name and title, as well as the industry and company size, in terms of both employee size and sales volume. The profiles also indicate whether a company is public or private, as well as detailed information regarding the company's products. There are a number of different search methods, including keyword searches by industry, SIC code, geographic area, or number of employees. This CD-ROM can be found in many university or public libraries, and is updated every six months.

Career Search—Integrated Resource System

21 Highland Circle, Needham, MA 02194-3075
617-449-0312

Career Search is a database that contains listings for over 700,000 privately and publicly held companies. You can find contact information, including names of human resources professionals or other executives, for companies of virtually all sizes, types, and industries. You can search the extensive database by keyword, industry, company size, or region. Updated monthly, this CD-ROM is available at colleges and universities, libraries, and some government agencies and career service companies.

Companies International

835 Penobscot Building, 645 Griswald Street, Detroit, MI 48226
800-877-GALE

Produced by Gale Research Inc., this database is geared more towards businesses than job hunters. However, you can still find plenty of valuable information within the database. The CD-ROM is compiled from *Ward's Business Directory* and the *World's Business Directory*, and contains information on more than 300,000 companies worldwide. Job seekers can find contact names, number of employees, and type of industry. Also included is information on the company's products and revenue. The database can be searched by industry, company products, or geographic location. Look for Companies International at your local public or university library.

CorpTech Directory

12 Alfred Street, Suite 200, Woburn, MA 01801-1915
800-333-8036

The CorpTech Directory on CD-ROM contains detailed descriptions of more than 45,000 mostly private, technology companies. It also lists the names and titles of nearly 155,000 executives—CEOs, sales managers, R & D managers, and human resources professionals, so job seekers can contact the appropriate managers within a given company. You can also find home page and email addresses. In addition to contact information, job seekers can find detailed information about the products the companies make, services they provide, and their annual sales revenue. The CorpTech Directory also provides an easy way to determine the growth of the company; it lists not only the number of current employees, but also the number of employees as of twelve months ago. Some companies also list the number of employees they expect to have in one year, so job seekers can see how much the company expects to grow. Job seekers can search the database by type of company, geographically, or by sales revenue. You can also create a more personalized search by entering in criteria for all fields. The producers of this database update it quarterly, and the directory can be found in many public and university libraries.

Duns Million Dollar Disc Plus
3 Sylvan Way, Parsippany, NJ 07054
800-526-0651
Compiled by Dun & Bradstreet, this CD-ROM lists information on over 420,000 companies. Of these, about 90 percent are privately held, but all have at least $3 million in annual sales or fifty employees. Dun's Million Dollar Disc is a broad directory, covering virtually every industry. The directory tells you the number of employees, sales volume, name of the parent company, and the corporate headquarters or branch locations. Of special interest to the job seeker is the inclusion of the names and titles of top executives, as well as biographical information, including education and career background. Searches can be done by location, industry, SIC code, or executive biography. This directory, which is updated quarterly, can be found at many colleges and universities, as well as at some public libraries.

Harris Complete
2057 Aurora Road, Twinsburg, OH 44087
800-888-5900
Produced by Harris InfoSource International, this directory of manufacturers profiles more than 300,000 companies. Although most companies are located in the United States, the directory also provides listings for some companies overseas. Besides contact infor-

mation, job seekers can find out the number of employees, plant size, and sales revenue. The database also contains the names and titles of over 600,000 top executives. Updated annually, the directory is available in CD-ROM format, and can be found in libraries, universities, or the offices of executive recruiters. The directory is also available in smaller regional or state editions.

Hoover's Handbook on CD-ROM
1033 La Posada Drive, Suite 50, Austin, TX 78752
512-454-7778
Published by Hoover's Inc., Hoover's Handbook on CD-ROM actually includes four different handbooks on one CD-ROM, and gives in-depth profiles of more than 2,500 companies and 200 industries. The database is only a subset of its print directory, but the information is much more thorough than the print version. The in-depth corporate profiles include detailed information on the company history, products, and growth prospects. The profiles also include information taken from the company's financial statements. The industry profiles include information on industry averages and projected growth for the industry. Updated quarterly, Hoover's Handbook on CD-ROM can be found at most public and university libraries.

Martindale-Hubbell Law Directory
121 Chanlon Road, New Providence, NJ 07974
800-526-4902
As the name says, this is a directory consisting exclusively of the names of legal employers. In all, the database has listings for over 900,000 lawyers and law firms. In addition to information regarding firms and practices, the database includes the biographies of many individual lawyers in the database. Thus, you can do searches by area of practice, firm name, law school attended, and field of law. While it lists some foreign law firms, the database consists predominantly of firms

in the U.S. This CD-ROM database is available to job seekers in most law libraries, as well as some university and public libraries.

Moody's Company Data
99 Church Street, New York, NY 10007
800-342-5647
Moody's Company Data is a CD-ROM that has detailed listings for over 11,000 leading publicly traded companies. In addition to information such as industry, company address, or phone and fax numbers, each listing includes the names and titles of top officers, including the CEO, president, and vice president, company size, number of shareholders, a corporate history, subsidiaries, and financial statements. Job seekers can conduct searches by region, SIC code, industry, or earnings. Updated monthly, this CD-ROM is available at public and university libraries, as well as the offices of some outplacement specialists.

Standard & Poor's Register
65 Broadway, New York, NY 10006
800-221-5277
The CD-ROM version of this three-volume desk reference provides job seekers with the same valuable information as its printed companion. The database lists over 55,000 top companies, including more than 12,000 public companies. In addition to contact information, which includes the names and titles of over 500,000 executives, you can find out about a company's primary and secondary sources of business, annual revenue, and number of employees, as well as parent company or subsidiaries. When available, the Register also lists the names of the company's bank, accounting, and law firms. Also, the directory provides extensive biographies of more than 70,000 top executives, which includes information such as directorships held and schools attended. There are fifty-five different search modes available on the database. Job seekers can search geographically, by zip code (either five or three digit), industry, SIC code, or

stock symbol. You can also request a search of only private or only public companies. Updated quarterly, this directory can be found in many colleges, universities, and public libraries.

Researching a Company for a Job Interview

Once you have scheduled an interview with a targeted company, you will need to begin your in-depth research. In order to prepare yourself for an interview, you need to know the company's products, types of customers, subsidiaries, parent company, corporate headquarters or regional locations, rank in the industry, sales and profit trends, whether the company is publicly or privately held, and current plans. You need to find out everything you can about the industry, the firm's principal competitors and their relative performance, and the direction in which the industry and its leaders are headed.

While many electronic employer databases will give you much of this information, you also need to take your research a step further. **Reading relevant articles about the company or the industry will enable you to enter your interview with more confidence.** Plus, the interviewer will be impressed if you are able to speak intelligently about industry trends or about the company's future plans.

But unless you are interviewing with a high profile company like Nike or Microsoft, company and industry news can be hard to find. This is especially true if you have an interview in a distant city or state, where you are less likely to have access to local information. **Business periodical databases** can contain hundreds of thousands of articles on business and industry. Most contain either full articles or abstracts (summaries) from hundreds of national, regional, and local business publications. From these articles, you can learn about what products a company is developing, marketing strategies, personnel moves, and financial condition—all the information you should know for an interview. Since these databases are updated as often as once a month, you will be sure to find the most current information. At the same time, you can also find articles dating back one or two years, which allows you to track the performance of a particular company over time. Other databases contain financial statements, Securities and Exchange Commission filings, or press releases from individual companies.

Like electronic employer databases, you can search business periodical databases in a number of ways: by company name, industry, region, or topic. Conducting a topic or industry search can often be a way to learn valuable information about a company's market share and competitors. By simply pressing a few keys, you can get a wealth of information—articles, press releases, and industry reports—about a company or industry. And of course, you can find this information in just a fraction of the time it took for you to find it before the advent of CD-ROM technology.

Look for these business periodical databases at your local public library. Again, not every library will have every database. Call to determine what resources are available, or to find out where you can get these resources. Most colleges and university libraries carry them as well.

Business Periodical Databases

ABI/Inform
300 North Zeeb Road, Ann Arbor, MI 48106
800-521-0600
Produced by UMI Corporation, this CD-ROM database contains abstracts from over 1,000 national business periodicals, including business, management, industry, and trade publications. This database is helpful to job seekers looking for information on a national level about hundreds of different industries. You can find information regarding industry trends, business conditions, products and services, and a number of other topics. The abstracts range in length from 25 to 150 words, and contain bib-

liographic citations, so you can easily find more in-depth information. ABI/Inform can be searched by company, industry, topic, or region, and is available at many public or university libraries. The database is updated each month, so you can be sure you are getting the most current business information.

Business and Company ProFile

362 Lakeside Drive, Foster City, CA 94404
800-419-0313

This comprehensive database contains information on business topics such as management, international business, business law, mergers and acquisitions, marketing and advertising, small and emerging companies, and new technologies and products. The database also contains directory information (name, address, phone number, and more) for more than 180,000 public and private companies. It contains abstracts of approximately 900 business periodicals, including full text for 460 of those. Some of the journals included are *The Wall Street Journal*, *The New York Times* financial section, local business journals, and economic publications, as well as trade publications in every industry segment that report on developments at over 50,000 companies. The database can be searched by keywords or subject. The company's sales office is located at One Park Avenue, 16th Floor, New York, NY 10016.

Business Dateline Ondisc

300 North Zeeb Road, Ann Arbor, MI 48106
800-521-0600

Made by UMI Corporation, the creators of ABI/Inform, Business Dateline Ondisc is the only source for regional and local business news. The database contains full articles from more than 450 local and regional publications, including the business sections of local daily newspapers, and business news wire services. Job seekers can learn in great detail about the growth prospects for smaller, local companies in a wide range of industries, as well as the economic outlook for the region or state. The database helps job seekers target a particular area that's experiencing solid growth, and determine which particular companies are hiring and expanding. Updated monthly, the database can be searched by company, industry, region, or topic, and can be found in many public or university libraries.

Investext on InfoTrac
362 Lakeside Drive, Foster City, CA 94404
800-419-0313
Compiled by the Information Access Company, the same company that produces Business and Company ProFile, the Investext database is a valuable resources for job hunters searching for detailed financial information about a particular company. Job hunters can use the database to analyze a company's line of business, locate current and historical financial information, or perform competitive analysis on products and companies. The database contains indexing and full text of more than 50,000 company and industry reports on more than 11,000 U.S. and international companies, and is searchable by both subject and keywords. The reports are compiled by 300 leading Wall Street, regional, and international brokerage, investment bank, and research firms in the U.S., Canada, Europe, and Asia.

CHAPTER ELEVEN

RESEARCHING COMPANIES ONLINE

As discussed in the previous chapter, investigating potential employers is crucial to the job hunting process. Whether you are researching companies to target in your job search or trying to educate yourself about a company's background for a job interview, it is essential to have thorough, up-to-date information on your target companies. And the best way to find this information is to use employer or other business databases. Once available only in unwieldy, printed volumes, this information is now widely available on CD-ROMs or, increasingly, online.

The type of company information you can find online varies widely, from the telephone book style of the Web's "Big Book" to the detailed financial reports found in Dun & Bradstreet's Business Reports through CompuServe. Some information comes in the form of employer databases like the CD-ROMs discussed in the previous chapter, where you can conduct searches according to criteria such as geographic location and industry. Many Web sites simply contain a list of companies with links to each company's own home page. General job hunting sites, like the Monster Board, include employer profiles of those companies with job listings at the site. Other databases, both on the Web and through commercial online services, contain much more in-depth information regarding a company's history, financial standing, or its products and services.

If you have a relatively short list of target companies you would like to learn more about, another option is to simply check out each company's home page on the Web. Companies of all sizes and in all industries are constantly popping up on the Web. Since most sites are geared toward consumers, most individual company Web sites include detailed information regarding the company's products and services. Others might include a company history; a list of company officers; financial information, such as historical stock performance or financial statements; and—of special interest to job hunters—employment information!

The Internet and commercial online services are also excellent resources for researching companies in periodicals. Today, most of the country's largest newspapers (including the *New York Times* and the *Wall Street Journal*), as well as magazines, trade publications, and regional business periodicals, have online versions of their publications. Many have their own Web sites, or are available through an online service like The Microsoft Network or America Online. If you are looking for information on a particular company, you can simply type in the company name, and search the publication for references to that company. Many publications even allow you to search their archives going back as many as three years.

The databases you choose to search will depend upon what information you are seeking. If you would simply like to find a list of all financial consulting firms in Chicago, a database like the Web's Big Book is most likely adequate. But if you are preparing for a job interview as a high-level financial analyst, you need to have a solid grasp of the company's finances. You can easily gather that type of information through a service like Dun & Bradstreet.

You may often find that companies are listed in two or more databases. You may be tempted to simply disregard the additional information and move on to a company you don't have information about. However, it's wise to compare the information contained in the different databases. If the information is consistent, then it's probably safe to assume that it's correct; if the two sources conflict, you should try to find a third source to determine which information is correct. It's also likely that many databases will contain different information; one may have financial information, and another may have a list of the chief executives. You should also take care to watch the timeliness of the information you are finding; while most online databases are updated frequently, that is not always the case.

Most information regarding companies and employers is found on the World Wide Web or through commercial online services like America Online and CompuServe. CompuServe in particular has many excellent resources for researching both national and international companies. Usenet newsgroups, Telnet, or Gopher sites, though extremely helpful in other areas of job hunting, generally contain little information that would be useful in researching companies and potential employers.

There are many advantages to researching companies online. The first is convenience; you can search right from your own home, instead of going to the library or employment service to use their information. Similarly, you can research companies whenever it's convenient to you; the Internet is available twenty-four hours a day. This convenience is especially valuable for last-minute job interviews. For instance, say you receive a call at three o'clock, asking you to come in for an interview the next day. In the past, you might have panicked because you wouldn't have had adequate time for research. But with the Internet, the information is right at your fingertips. Also, the information on the Internet is generally more current than what you can find on CD-ROMs or in books, with many companies updating their information daily. Finally, researching companies can go much faster on the Internet. Once you know where to look, the information is only a few keystrokes away. You no longer have to carve out a large part of your day to go to the library and do research.

As for disadvantages, well, there really aren't that many. In most cases, accessing this information is free (except for your online monthly charges, of course). And while some services—especially those found only on commercial online services—charge for accessing some information, there's generally enough free information out there so looking in fee-based databases is not always necessary. If you do have to enter a fee-based area, just think of how valuable that knowledge is, especially for job interviews.

Researching Employers on the Web

New resources for researching potential employers are popping up regularly on the World Wide Web. To find additional resources, use a search engine like Yahoo! or AltaVista, and type in the keyword "companies" or "employers." You can also tap into job hunting Meta-lists, such as Purdue University's Placement Services-Internet Sites for Job Seekers and Employers (**http://www.purdue.edu/student/jobsites.htm**), which provides links to numerous other career resources.

Listed below are several examples of databases that can be used to search for employers. These databases can be accessed free of charge, although there are several others that do charge small fees for searches.

America's Employers
http://www.americasemployers.com
The philosophy behind America's Employers is that since most job openings are never advertised, the best way to find jobs is through direct contact with targeted companies. This extensive database has a search engine that allows you to search by state (either alone or in combination with another state), industry, or company name. America's Employers doesn't really give you in-depth information about a particular company; instead you will simply find names, addresses, and telephone numbers. It does provide links to each listed company's Web site when applicable.

Big Book
http://www.bigbook.com

While not specifically designed for job hunters, Big Book contains the names, addresses, and phone numbers of hundreds of thousands of businesses throughout the country. You can search the extensive database by category, state, and city. Big Book can be tremendously useful for job interviews: By selecting a particular company in your targeted list, you'll see a detailed map of the area near the business, with the company's exact location highlighted. Big Book also allows you to select companies and insert them into your own personalized "little book" of companies.

CareerCity
http://www.careercity.com

To reach the company profiles, choose the "Jobs Database" link from the main page and then select "Corporate Recruiting Links." CareerCity's company recruiting links search engine covers over 700 companies, with names, addresses, phone numbers, and brief descriptions available. The employers are searchable by industry and by geographic region, and the listings feature direct links to each company's home page.

CareerMagazine
http://www.careermag.com

To reach the detailed company profiles contained here, select "Employer Profiles" from the main menu, which provides a list of over 100 companies to choose from. Click on a specific company and you will see in-depth information regarding a company's structure, philosophy, and number of employees. While you can't do an actual search of a specific company in your city or field, CareerMagazine does provide an employer directory with brief summaries of each company.

CareerMosaic
http://www.careermosaic.com

CareerMosaic's employer database contains over two hundred large companies with more being added every day. Unfortunately, you cannot conduct a true search—you must look at lists of employers and then choose the one you want. The list of employers acts as a link to each company's home page; therefore, the information you find on a given company will depend on the content of its home page.

Company Profiles
http://www.jobtrak.com

Company Profiles contains a listing (with links) of hundreds of companies. The list is arranged alphabetically, so you can simply scroll down the list and select your targeted companies. Of course, the information you find will depend on the content of a company's Web site. But what you're likely to find is information about the company's history, products and services, and maybe even employment opportunities. While you're here, you should also check out the file, "Researching Employers on the Web" (**http://www.jobtrak.com/jobsearch_docs.employer_lists.html**). Here you will find links to additional resources for researching employers.

E-Span's Interactive Employment Network
http://www.espan.com

Again, you must choose "Employer Profiles" from the opening menu to find this information. As on CareerMosaic, E-Span's employer profiles are presented as a list of links to each company's home page, so the information you find will depend on what's on each company's home page.

EDGAR Database of Corporate Information
http://www.sec.gov/edgarhp.htm

EDGAR, or the Electronic Data Gathering, Analysis, and Retrieval system, is the electronic filing arm of the Securities and Exchange Commission (SEC). All publicly traded companies, and many others, are required by law to file certain documents with the SEC. Some international companies also file with EDGAR, but this is not mandatory. Job hunters can search the database for specific companies, and are likely to find information such as forms 10K and 10Q (annual and quarterly reports), as well as Form 144 (notice of proposed sale of securities) and other financial information.

Job Web
http://www.jobweb.com

To access, choose "Employer Directory" from the main menu. You can search the database of companies by keyword or by state. Choose a particular company from your search results, and you will find a description of the company, along with its philosophy, and a summary of available job opportunities.

Lexis-Nexis
http://www.lexis-nexis.com

Unfortunately, the granddaddy of all business databases is not available on the Web. It's still available only through Telnet, and only for a very substantial fee, since the company is marketed to institutional customers. But the site does provide valuable information on the various databases Lexis-Nexis offers, as well as phone numbers to give you additional information. Also, many companies and institutions, including libraries, have access to certain Lexis-Nexis databases. Thus, you may be able to gain access to Lexis-Nexis through your online services at work Their site indicates that they have over *one billion* documents available!

The Monster Board
http://www.monster.com

This graphically entertaining site contains "online brochures" for 350 employers worldwide. To narrow your prospects, you can search by geographic location (including Canada). Each company's profile includes information on products and services, benefits, and corporate culture and environment. Some profiles include a link that allows you to search for job opportunities in a particular company.

Student Center
http://www.studentcenter.com

Although this site is designed to give college students and recent graduates career advice and direction, it also provides a database of over 35,000 companies. You can search the database by keywords, by state, or by area code, so it's easy to pinpoint those companies in your geographic area that match your interests and field. The search results tell you the name, address, and telephone number of the company, along with a brief explanation of the company's industry.

Researching Employers through Commercial Online Services

Services like America Online and CompuServe are gold mines of valuable information for job seekers. Job hunters can find detailed information that helps them target potential employers or prepare for job interviews. Costs of the services will vary. Most databases on CompuServe charge a search fee in addition to the CompuServe connect time charges. It typically costs around $45 to obtain full company profiles for five companies. America Online, on the other hand, has a smaller selection of business resources, but the information is available free of charge. Many job seekers may find they don't really need the in-depth financial information that many of the more expensive databases on CompuServe provide.

America Online

American Business Information/American Yellow Pages
Keyword: ABI

Like the name implies, ABI provides the basic name, address, and phone number for thousands of companies. It also gives a "credit score" for each company, which is calculated using a "multi-variable computer-regression model." The variables considered include number of employees, years in business, and industry stability. Unfortunately, you can't see any of that information; you must rely on the credit score to get an indication of that. There is no charge for searching the American Yellow Pages.

Hoover's Business Resources

Keyword: hoover

Calling itself "The Ultimate Source for Company Information," Hoover provides profiles for over 9,800 companies, including information on company officers, annual sales, and number of employees. Each company profile even allows you to search the Web for references to the specific company. You can also find information on the top fifty companies for selected U.S. cities such as Atlanta, Boston, and Los Angeles; which companies are in the Fortune 500; and links to over 2,000 corporate Web sites. Searching the database carries no fees in addition to the connect time charges from America Online.

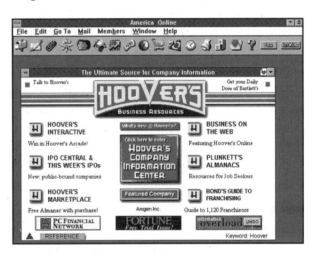

CompuServe

Business Database Plus

Go: busdb

This database contains five years' worth of articles from over 750 business magazines, trade journals, and regional business newspapers. You can also find articles—dating back two years—from more than 500 specialized business newsletters. Updated weekly, this comprehensive database can provide you with timely, in-depth information on business and industry trends from throughout the world. The database also contains detailed company profiles and industry descriptions. In addition to CompuServe charges, there's a $.25 per minute surcharge, but there's no charge for reading or downloading articles.

Corporate Affiliations
Go: affiliations

This extensive database contains company profiles for most large public and private companies and their subsidiaries. A company profile can contain an address, phone number, and description, as well as names of directors and executives, total sales, assets, net worth, liabilities, and if applicable, what exchange the company's stock is traded on. Some listings also contain the corporate family structure, parent company name and location, and more. Published by the National Register Publishing Company and made available by Dialog Information Services, Corporate Affiliations charges $5 per search, with additional charges for other services. These charges, in combination with the connect charges from CompuServe, can add up to some pretty hefty research fees.

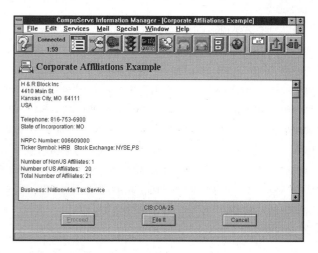

Disclosure SEC

Go: disclosure

Job hunters scanning the Disclosure database can find financial information for over 10,500 companies. The information is gathered from the 10K (annual) and 10Q (quarterly) documents that publicly traded companies are required to file with the Securities and Exchange Commission. Among the most valuable resources for a job hunter is the management discussion, which generally indicates the future direction and financial health of a company. You will also find annual income statements, balance sheets, and ratio reports (some going back as far as eight years); quarterly income statements; ownership information (including the names, holdings, and transactions of the company's principals and institutions); the letter the president sends to all shareholders; and more. Charges for reports vary, depending on how much information you want. There's no charge for a company's name and address, but it costs $5 for a company profile and $11 for a company's financial statements. However, you can get all reports, including the company profile, financial statements, management discussion, president's letter, officers, and directors, for only $17.

Dun's Electronic Business Directory

Go: dunsebd

Dun's database provides directory information on over eight million U.S. businesses and individuals, including both public and private companies of all sizes and types. Company information includes the address, telephone number, type of business, number of employees, industry, SIC code, and Dun's number. An entry for an individual most likely will not contain all this information. In addition to CompuServe's connection charges, you'll spend $7.50 for a search that retrieves up to five companies, and an additional $7.50 for five more companies. Full company references are extra, and searches that yield no results will cost $1.

Dun & Bradstreet Online

Go: duns

Dun & Bradstreet Online contains six additional databases that yield more substantial information than what you'll find in Dun's Electronic Business Directory. These databases contain directory information on almost 12.5 million U.S., Canadian, and international companies, as well as business reports with financial information on additional companies. Again, these databases carry transaction charges in addition to the regular CompuServe fees. Charges range from $7.50 for a search of Dun's Market Identifiers, to $100 for a copy of the financial records and summary financial for a European company in Dun's Financial Records Plus Summary Financials.

- **D & B Dun's FRP History/Operations Reports.** Covers over 1.8 million publicly and privately held U.S. companies and 2.4 million Western European businesses. In addition to company names, addresses, and telephone numbers, you can find sales figures, number of employees, date of incorporation, corporate family hierarchy, and name of the chief executive. For U.S. companies, you will also find a short company history. Expect to pay $10 for your search, $50 for a full company report ($25 for a European company).

- **D & B Dun's FRP Summary/Financials Reports.** Only look at this database if you are researching European companies, because the information for U.S. companies is the same as that found in Dun's FRP History/Operations Reports. For European companies, however, you will also find a financial summary that includes total assets, liabilities, and net worth. Again, you'll pay $10 for a search, which can yield up to five companies, and $75 for a full company report ($100 for a European company).

- **D & B Dun's Market Identifiers.** Contains information on more than ten million U.S. companies (both public and private), government organizations, and schools and universities. You'll find the name, address, and telephone number for all companies. Other information you are likely to find for most companies includes sales revenue, number of employees, net worth, incorporation dates, and names and titles of company executives and officers. Searches cost $7.50, plus another $7.50 for each full reference.

- **D & B Dun's Canadian Market Identifiers.** Information covers about 350,000 Canadian companies. Listings include name, address, telephone number, sales revenue, and name of the chief executive officer. Cost is the same as that for Dun's Domestic Market Identifiers.

- **D & B Dun's International Market Identifiers.** Contains information on over 2.1 million public, private, and government-controlled companies in Asia, Africa, Europe, the Middle East, South America, Australia, and the Pacific Rim—120 countries in all. Most entries include name, address, telephone number, cable or telex number, type of business, size (by number of employees and sales), name of the chief executive, and the parent company name.

- **Dun & Bradstreet Business Reports.** Includes three types of financial and credit reports containing information on over ten million companies. These reports are the Business and Information Report, the Payment Analysis Report, and the Supplier Evaluation Report. The reports contain such information as the Dun & Bradstreet rating, company history, payment filings, public filings, and other financial information. While there's no charge for a search that retrieves no results, fees for successfully retrieved reports range from $49.50 to $92.50.

InvesText
Go: invtext

Here, job hunters will find in-depth reports on more than 8,200 public U.S. companies and over 2,300 public foreign corporations, as well as industry reports for over fifty industry groups, such as consumer goods and services, real estate, and finance. Compiled by fifty leading Wall Street, regional, and international brokerage houses and research firms, the reports contain company profiles and a detailed financial history including revenues, earnings, stock performance, and an analysis and projection of future performance. Costs range from $7.50 for a search by topic or report number to $20 for a report title search. Full page citations also cost $15 each.

Thomas Register Online
Go: thomas

Thomas Register provides job hunters with profiles for almost 150,000 U.S. and Canadian manufacturers and service providers. Each record contains the company name, address, and telephone number, and the type of products or services provided. Some records also contain number of employees, names and titles of chief executives, names of parent or subsidiary companies, asset rating, and more. Searches cost $7.50 to retrieve up to five companies, $7.50 for each additional set of five companies, and $7.50 to view a full company record.

Searching for Company Web Sites

As mentioned earlier, a company's home page on the World Wide Web is often one of the best sources of information for job hunters. You can learn the company history and read the company's mission statement, which generally provides the names of its chief executives. Many sites for larger, public companies include information for stockholders, like financial statements, annual reports, earnings reports, and stock quotes. Many Web sites also contain press releases where you can read about recent developments within the company, such as new product launches, changes among executives, or other important information.

The tone of a home page can also be a good way to get a feel for the company's corporate culture. For instance, Ben & Jerry's lighthearted depiction of cows and dancing skeletons is consistent with the laid-back, easy-going culture that the company promotes. Arthur Anderson's home page, on the other hand, has a professionalism and polish that is appropriate for an international Big Six accounting firm.

For many job hunters, however, the most valuable information to be found on a home page is employment information. Many of this country's leading employers, from Adobe Systems, Inc. to Wal-Mart, post job listings on their home pages. Home pages that don't contain job listings usually include some general information on how to apply for a job, such as a street or email address. Others go into a little more detail, outlining requirements for some common positions and describing the departments within the company. In either case, this is usually more information than you can get from most employer databases, or from speaking to a human resources representative within a company.

In effect, looking at a company's Web page amounts to one-stop shopping for job hunters. Instead of calling companies for annual reports, searching through executive directories for the name of the second vice-president of marketing, and poring over old business periodicals looking for news regarding a potential employer, you can simply log on to the company's Web page and find this information. Of course, the content of each company's home page will vary—there is no uniformity to sites on the World Wide Web. Some sites have more information than you could possibly need, while others only skim the surface.

Unfortunately, you can't simply look up a company's URL in the telephone book, like you can an address or telephone number. Luckily, however, you can use large Web search engines and directories to find the URLs of thousands of companies. The following list should help you get started:

Career Resource Center
http://www.careers.org
This Meta-list of job hunting resources contains over 17,000 links to employers, job listings, reference materials, and more. The Employers Links section has links to more than 5,000 companies. You can either perform a search of all companies or browse through the more manageable category lists, such as technology companies or financial services. Companies include Ciba-Geigy (**http://www.ciba.com**) and Digital Equipment (**http://www.digital.com**).

Excite
http://www.excite.com/xdr/Business/Companies
The Excite search engine will give you a directory of thousands of companies in all industry categories. The directory, which includes summaries describing the sites, puts companies in categories like "Computers & Internet," which is where 3Com (**http://www.3com.com**) is listed. You are linked directly to the Web sites simply by selecting the company name from the directory.

JobHunt
http://www.job-hunt.org
Another Meta-list of job hunting resources available on the Internet, this site contains a list of companies that post job openings on their Web sites. The list includes links to dozens of companies like Procter & Gamble (**http://www.pg.com**) and Sun Microsystems (**http://www.sun.com**). JobHunt also contains lists of resume banks, reference materials, and job listings.

Magellan
http://www.mckinley.com
Choose "Business" from the main menu of the Magellan search engine, and then choose "Companies." You'll find a directory of over 550 links to companies such as Ben & Jerry's Homemade, Inc.

(**http://www.benjerry.com**) and Colgate-Palmolive Company (**http://www.colgate.com**). The directory also includes short reviews of the sites so you have an idea of what you'll find when you get there. Magellan is a subsidiary of the previously mentioned Excite, Inc., which can also be accessed through this site.

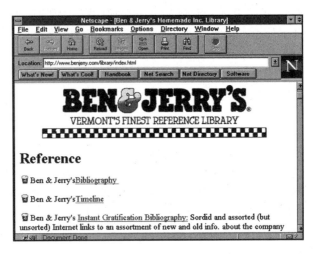

Open Market's Commercial Sites Index
http://www.directory.net
This huge site contains the names of over 35,000 companies, commercial services, products, and information that can be accessed through the Internet. Since the information is so dense, you can perform a keyword search to find what you're looking for. If you have a few particular companies in mind, you can also search the list alphabetically. Each listing is a link to that particular company's (or service's or product's) Web site. Frito-Lay (**http://www.fritolay.com**) is just one of the companies listed in this index.

Yahoo!
http://www.yahoo.com/text/Business_and_Economy/Companies/
Like Magellan and Excite, Yahoo!'s search engine is a standout resource for company information. The site has thousands of links

to companies in dozens of categories—accounting, advertising, computers, consulting—you name it. Among the companies you'll find links to are Johnson & Johnson (**http://www.jnj.com**) and Reebok (**http://www.reebok.com**). You can also easily search for firms in your field by simply typing in keywords like "health care." Or, you can search for a specific company simply by using the company name in your keyword search.

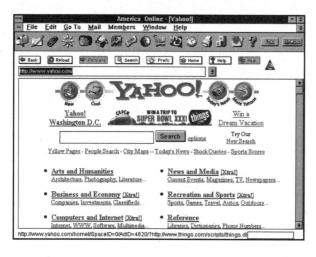

CHAPTER TWELVE

NETWORKING ONLINE

A sk anyone in the employment industry—consultants, outplacement specialists, human resources professionals—and they will probably tell you that the best way to find a job is through networking. In fact, **one common figure tossed around employment circles is that *eighty percent* of all jobs are found through networking.** Not by contacting employers directly, not through employment agencies, and not through the newspaper help-wanted ads. Therefore, establishing a solid, extensive network of contacts within your field of interest should be a top priority.

While some may think that top executives and industry insiders are the only people to benefit from networking, that is not the case. The development of specialized online discussion groups has made it easier for all job hunters to meet and interact with other professionals in the same field or industry. Every day, thousands of job hunters log on to the Internet's Usenet discussion groups or mailing lists, or visit the special interest groups (SIGs) on commercial online services in order to discuss issues and developments relevant to the field, compare experiences, or exchange information, including employment opportunities.

Usenet discussion groups, mailing lists, and SIGs are ideal for networking since they were designed so that people interested in the same things could discuss their similar interests by posting and reading messages. Today, there are hundreds of online discussion groups on virtually any topic, ranging from religion to politics to popular TV shows. The dozens of career-related discussion groups available cover fields like accounting, education, journalism, and microbiology.

The main objective of networking is to become visible to prospective employers. Other benefits of online networking include:

- **Discussion group participants often include human resources representatives and hiring managers,** who often lend their expertise by discussing the qualities they look for in employees. And, many recruiters report visiting field-specific discussion groups to look for potential job candidates.

- **Participating in online discussion groups brings far greater exposure than, for instance, going to a meeting of a local industry group.** A discussion group's audience is most often nationwide, and may even include participants from around the world.

- **Monitoring discussion groups makes it easy to determine what skills and experiences employers are looking for.** For instance, do most of the other participants have their MBAs? It's also a good way to find out which companies are hiring and what are the hot topics and issues in the field.

Job hunters should look at three main areas as potential networking resources: Usenet newsgroups, mailing lists, and special interest groups on commercial online services. Gopher, Telnet, and the World Wide Web do not lend themselves well to networking since they were not designed for two-way communication. Newsgroups, mailing lists, and SIGs, on the other hand, were designed expressly for the purpose of disseminating and receiving information. At the same time, keep an eye out for Web sites of industry organizations and associations. At last count, the Web had over 130 sites dedicated to specific fields or industries. While they do not have the ability to accept posted messages, field-specific Web sites are still a good way to keep up with the latest developments and advances in a particular field, and to keep abreast of the hot issues in that field.

Do not expect to be besieged with job offers and contact names simply because you logged on to a professional discussion group and posted a message full of intelligence and insight. Networking online is a slow process, since in the online world, just as in real life, relationships do not form overnight, and it takes time to build up trusted contacts. In fact, it may be months before any job leads materialize. That's why we suggest continually maintaining a presence in appropriate discussion groups—even when you are happily employed—since the opportunity of a lifetime may turn up when it's least expected.

The Importance of Netiquette

"Netiquette" is simply a combination of the words "network" (or Internet) and "etiquette." Originally used to describe the rules surrounding Usenet newsgroups, netiquette now refers to the widely accepted do's and don'ts for using any type of online discussion group. It is essential that new users, or "newbies," are familiar with the netiquette of a group before joining the discussion; otherwise, they might get "flamed" (criticized and ridiculed by established group members).

The easiest way to avoid getting flamed is to spend time observing and reading the group's posted messages *before* attempting to join the discussion. Each discussion group, especially those on Usenet, have a particular tone and rules. Simply "lurking" (reading messages but not posting your own) in a particular group will give you a good sense of the group's personality. This is also a good way to ensure that a particular group will really fit your interests.

When you are ready to join in the discussion, don't simply post a general message along the lines of, "Hi, I'm new here and just wanted to drop in and say hello!" Post a message asking for specific advice, or introduce an original thought or comment to the discussion. A boring, generic posting with headers like "Help!" or "Hire Me!" will be ignored at best, and will get you flamed at worst. If you do get flamed—something that is bound to happen to every new user once or twice—just ignore it. Unless you violated a sacred rule of netiquette, someone was probably just having a bad day.

Following are some other basic rules of netiquette, as well as some general guidelines to follow in professional discussion groups:

- **In all postings, write in full and complete sentences,** and be sure that all spelling, punctuation, grammar, and capitalization are correct.
- **Don't type messages in all capital letters** because that's the online equivalent of SHOUTING.
- **Don't use "emoticons" such as** :) (happy face), or : ((frown), or common abbreviations like BTW (By The Way) and IMHO (In My Humble Opinion) which are commonly used in recreational discussion groups. These types of cutesy shorthand are out of place in a professional discussion group, and if you want to be taken seriously, don't use them.
- **Understand the appropriate times to post or email a reply to a particular message.** Many new and experienced users alike are often unsure of when to direct an email to the message's author, and when a reply should be posted to the group. In general, post a reply if your message is something the group as a whole could appreciate and learn from, but use email if your comment only con-

cerns the poster. This is important because no one wants to participate in a discussion that is little more than a dialogue between two or three people.

- **Finally, use your best manners.** Respect and be tolerant of others' ideas and opinions.

Networking on Usenet Newsgroups

Newsgroups are a terrific place for networking, with discussion groups to suit almost every interest. Newsgroups also tend to have the harshest rules of netiquette, due in part to the fact that—since newsgroups are one of the oldest areas of the Internet—their participants are more technologically savvy than the online world as a whole. At the same time, their users are extremely knowledgeable, and helpful to those who have taken the time to learn the rules. Some locations for you to get started include the following:

alt.journalism.moderated
Moderated discussion group for journalists.

ba.jobs.misc
Discusses the job market in the San Francisco Bay area.

bionet.women-in-bio
Discusses issues relevant to women in the field of biology.

bionet.microbiology
Discussion of issues related to microbiology.

hepnet.jobs
Discussion of issues relating to high-energy nuclear physics.

il.jobs.misc
Discussion of the job market in Illinois.

k12.chat.teacher

Discussion group for teachers of all grades, from kindergarten
 to the twelfth grade.

misc.business.consulting

Discusses the consulting business.

misc.education

General discussion of the educational system.

misc.jobs.contract

Discussion of both short- and long-term contract labor.

misc.jobs.misc

General issues of employment and careers are discussed.

misc.legal

Discussion group for lawyers and others involved in the legal
 profession.

misc.writing

A discussion group for writers of all types.

nyc.jobs.misc

Discussion of the New York City job market.

rec.arts.books

Discussion of all types of books, as well as the field of
 publishing.

sat.jobs

Discussion of the San Antonio, Texas job market.

sci.med

Discussion group for those interested in science and medicine.

sci.med.pharmacy

Discusses the pharmaceutical field.

sci.research.careers

Discusses the various careers relating to scientific research.

Networking with Mailing Lists

Mailing lists, also known as list-serves or email discussion groups, are like a cousin to Usenet discussion groups. Like newsgroups, mailing lists allow users to post and read messages that contain threads of discussions on various topics. What sets mailing lists apart from newsgroups is that instead of users logging in to a specific group and posting and reading messages online, sub-scribers automatically receive new messages, and post messages to the group, via email. Many users like mailing lists because they allow users to monitor discussion groups simply by checking their email, which is something most of us do everyday.

To subscribe to a mailing list, send an email to the list's system administrator. The list administrator makes sure that all messages are sent to subscribers, and moderates the content, ensuring that postings are relevant to the topic. Like other discussion groups, each mailing list has its own rules and guidelines, so be sure to contact the list's administrator for details.

There are tens of thousands of mailing lists available, cover-ing subjects like arts, business, health, politics, and religion. To find the mailing lists that match your interests, consult the selec-tion of online directories that follow. Each directory contains contact information, such as the system administrator's email address, for over 50,000 mailing lists.

Liszt: The Mailing List Directory
http://www.liszt.com

This directory claims to be the largest directory of mailing lists, and it just may be, with 71,618 lists available for searching. The site also allows you to search by keywords.

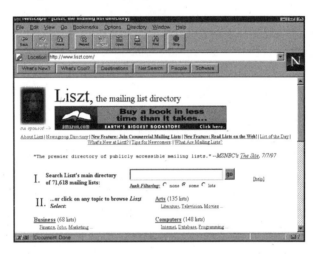

Publicly Accessible Mailing Lists
http://www.neosoft.com/internet/paml

Maintained by Stephanie da Silva, this list is searchable by name or subject. It contains hundreds of different subject classifications. Check under "jobs" or "employment" for job-related mailing lists, but check out lists in your field as well. This list is also posted to the Usenet newsgroups **news.lists** and **news.answers** around the end of each month.

Special Interest Groups (SIGs)

SIGs are found only on commercial online services, such as America Online, CompuServe, and Prodigy. SIGs, like newsgroups, are a means by which people with similar interests can gather online to exchange ideas and information. While these groups are called different names on each service—forums, bulletin boards (*not to be* confused with the *Bulletin Board Systems* discussed in Chapter 8), roundtables—they are known collectively as SIGs.

SIGs differ from newsgroups in a number of ways. First, SIGs have smaller audiences, because fewer people subscribe to commercial online services than have access to the Internet. Also, most SIGs have moderators, called sysops, or system operators, who monitor the discussions to be sure that the comments are relevant to the specific group. They also make sure that the discussions don't get out of hand, which despite netiquette, can occasionally happen (this is usually called a flame war). And in most special interest groups, the main subject is subdivided into smaller directories, which make it easy to pinpoint the exact topic you want to discuss.

Finally, keep in mind that the commercial online services provide their subscribers with full Internet access. Therefore, if you can't find a forum that fits your interests here, browse the newsgroups and mailing lists directories for a group that seems more appropriate.

America Online

In addition to this commercial online service's outstanding career resources (*please refer to the America Online section in Chapter 4*), America Online has a number of forums for networking with other professionals. Most of the services described in this section are not forums in the strictest sense, meaning that they offer other valuable information in addition to their message boards. To find a complete list of America Online special interest groups, search for the keywords "clubs" and "forums" in the Directory of Services.

Health Professionals Network
Keyword: HRS or Better Health
Choose "Health Professionals Network" from the main menu. The

Network contains over seventy-five topics for all types of health professionals, including physicians, physician assistants, and physical therapists.

Legal Information Network
Keyword: LIN
The Legal Information Network offers networking resources for paralegals, family law specialists, social security specialists, women lawyers, and law students.

P.L.A.C.E.S. Forum
Keyword: places
P.L.A.C.E.S. is a discussion group for professionals in the planning, landscape, architecture, construction, engineering, and specifications fields.

The Teacher's Lounge
Keyword: teacher's lounge
Allows teachers of kindergarten through the twelfth grade to trade ideas and discuss relevant issues.

Women's Network
Keyword: women
Through the Career Message Board, professional women can discuss issues such as job burnout and women in the workplace, or receive job hunting support and career counseling.

The Writers Club
Keyword: writers
This club offers writers the opportunity to exchange information, such as how to find a publisher or secure freelance work, and offers writing workshops and advice.

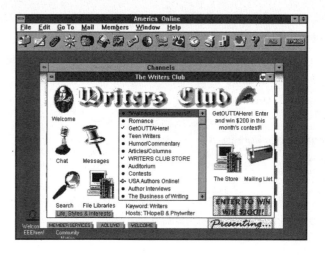

CompuServe

With over 900 forums, CompuServe has by far the most discussion groups for professionals, with forums in a wide range of fields. CompuServe is well-known for the quality of its forums and the participants therein. Its forums have three basic components: the message section, where users can post and read messages; conference areas that allow users to participate in real-time chats, as well as scheduled meetings or conferences with other users; and libraries, which enable users to search for archival information such as conference transcripts and articles related to the forum's topic. **Most forums require you to join them, but there is no fee for membership.** Often, forums may restrict access to nonmembers; in some forums, for instance, you may not have access to the libraries or conference rooms if you have not joined.

Following is a list of some of the best professional forums that CompuServe offers. To find additional forums, select Find from the Services menu, or click on the Index icon, and type in your desired subject area. You'll then be presented with a list of related forums.

AMIA/MedSIG
Go: MedSIG
Open to all professionals in the health care field to discuss medical issues and exchange information regarding such topics as new advances in medicine.

Accountants Forum
Go: Aicpa
Sponsored by the American Institute of Certified Public Accountants, this forum provides information for professionals interested in the field of accounting.

Architecture and Building Forum
Go: Arch
Allows for discussion and the exchange of information between architectural professionals.

Broadcast Professionals Forum
Go: BPForum
Allows for professionals in radio and television to share news and views about the industry.

Computer Consultants
Go: Consult
Allows computer professionals to discuss issues related to the field, including networking and business development.

Court Reporters Forum
Go: Crforum
Networking forum for court reporters that includes information from the National Court Reporters Association and the *Journal of Court Reporting*.

Desktop Publishing Forum
Go: Dtpforum
Discussion group for professionals in the field of electronic publishing, design, writing, and printing.

Education Forum
Go: Edforum
This forum is open to teachers at all levels, administrators, college and university personnel, as well as education publishers, for the discussion of issues relevant to education.

Information Management Forum
Go: Infomanage
Intended for all types and levels of information management professions, the forum contains information on related professional conferences and associations.

Journalism Forum
Go: Jforum
This group is a place for journalists of all kinds—print, radio, television, even freelancers. You can discuss issues of the day, look for jobs, and talk about the business of news.

NL Professionals Forum
Go: Nlprof
Written in both Dutch and English, this is *the* place to contact Dutch professionals and to look for a job in the Netherlands.

Photo Professionals
Go: Photopro
Imaging professionals and all those interested in entering the field are welcome to join in discussions regarding imaging and photography.

ProPublishing Forum

Go: Propub

Open to anyone in publishing or the graphic arts to discuss issues relating to the field. This forum charges a small monthly fee to its members.

Public Relations and Marketing Forum

Go: Prsig

This discussion group for marketing and PR professionals is great for networking and finding contacts. It also offers its members a huge library of information.

Travel Professionals Forum

Go: Travpro

This forum discusses topics relevant to the travel industry. It also has a "professionals only" area that includes information on networking. To join this area, you will need to send an email to the sysop for permission.

Writer's Forum

Go: Writers

Here, writers of all experience levels can make contacts, get advice, receive support, or have their work critiqued. This site is especially helpful for writers who are looking to break into freelancing.

Delphi

This small, text-based commercial service has three high-quality special interest groups for professionals. Delphi also has dozens of other Custom Forums on a wide range of topics. Plus, users have relatively easy access to Usenet newsgroups and the rest of the Internet.

Advertising/Marketing Professionals
Go: Custom 370
This is a discussion group open to advertising and marketing professionals of all kinds—print, television, direct mail, and more.

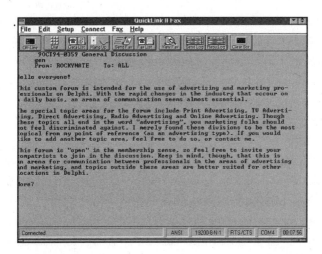

The Law Forum
Go: Custom 194
The forum allows lawyers and other legal professionals to discuss and debate issues pertaining to the law in all its forms.

Nursing Network Forum
Go: Custom 261
An electronic bulletin board where nurses can meet to discuss all aspects of nursing. The forum also has periodic "live" conferences with special guests.

The Microsoft Network

As was mentioned earlier, The Microsoft Network has been playing catch-up in many online service areas. However, there are two forums which are definitely worth checking out for jobseekers, described below.

Career Forum
Go: Careers
Career Forum features career chats, answers to specific questions, and advice from experts. Job hunting tips are also available.

Watercooler
Go: watercooler
Offering "career stories, career solutions," this inventive site provides suggestions, advice, and a variety of chats, relating to both job seeking and workplace issues.

Prodigy

Prodigy's special interest groups are called Bulletin Boards, which should not be confused with the dial-up Bulletin Board Systems (BBSs) described earlier. Prodigy offers dozens of Bulletin Boards for a wide range of topics, including several for professionals, and an all-purpose careers discussion group. To find a complete list of Bulletin Boards, click on the "BB" button on the toolbar at the bottom of the screen.

Books and Writing
Jump to: Books and Writing BB
The Books and Writing Bulletin Board is a place for writers to discuss the publishing business and writing techniques, as well as offer advice and criticism.

Careers
Jump to: Careers BB
This general site includes message areas for the fields of arts and entertainment, design, construction, engineering, and others. Job hunters can network and find advice from professionals in their field.

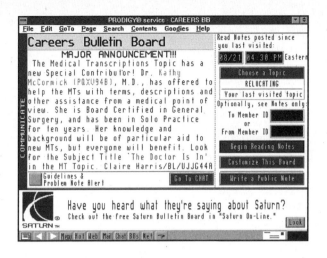

Education

Jump to: Education BB

Teachers of all grade levels can find advice and support, and discuss issues important to those involved in the education field.

Legal Exchange

Jump to: Legal Exchange

A forum for lawyers and others in the legal profession to debate and discuss important issues, such as those arising from widely publicized trials.

Your Business

Jump to: Your Business

This forum is dedicated to those who have started their own business. Small business owners discuss the challenges of running a small business, and offer advice and guidance for less experienced participants.

PART FOUR

OTHER ADVANCES IN ELECTRONIC JOB HUNTING

CHAPTER THIRTEEN

COMPUTER-ASSISTED JOB INTERVIEWS

Just when you thought the whole job search process couldn't get any more high-tech, along comes the computerized job interview. Many companies, especially those that regularly hire large numbers of employees, are now having candidates complete a computerized job interview in place of an initial screening interview with a human resources representative. Like the traditional screening interview, the computer asks the candidates questions regarding their work history, background, skills, and qualifications, usually in the true/false or multiple choice formats. Once the interview is complete, the computer provides the interviewer with a summary of the candidate's answers. Among other things, this summary might recommend bringing the candidate in for a face-to-face interview, and provide the interviewer with a list of follow-up questions for the second interview.

Candidates who have taken computer-assisted interviews give high marks to the computer; many report being less anxious and nervous during the interview. Human resources professionals like the system because it streamlines the hiring process and makes it more efficient. Companies that use computer-assisted job interviews report higher productivity, improved customer service, lower employee turnover and absenteeism, and less theft in the workplace.

Computerized job interviews are based on the principle of the structured job interview. Structured job interviews, which have long been valued by human resources professionals, are simply interviews where the same prescribed set of questions are asked of every candidate applying for positions within a company. (Of course, this is usually only used for the initial screening interviews; second interviews generally tend to be less structured and more of a conversation.) Advocates of the structured interview say that it brings a consistency and fairness to the hiring process that is lacking when nonstructured interviews are used. The standardized format of the interview allows recruiters to more easily compare candidates' responses—each candidate gets asked the same question phrased exactly the same way. Also, each question is carefully phrased so the interviewer doesn't have to worry about breaking any employment laws. One final advantage—structured interviews gather more information in less time than nonstructured interviews.

Brooks Mitchell, Ph.D., founder and president of Aspen Tree Software and a leader in the field of computer-assisted job interviews, was the first person to see how easily a computer could perform the initial screening interview. After all, he reasoned, what could be more consistent and impartial than a computer? Mitchell based his idea on the structured job interview, and in 1978, administered the first computer-assisted job interview in a large New Jersey plant. **Since then, the use of computer-assisted interviews has continued to grow in fields and companies that traditionally hire large volumes of workers, such as banks, hospitals, hotels, and retailers.** These types of companies can have hundreds of entry-level job openings each year, and since employers typically interview as many as ten candidates for a single position, the computer-assisted interview can greatly increase the efficiency of the hiring process. Since the computer screens out any unqualified candidates, the hiring manager spends time only with those candidates who have the skills and qualifications necessary for the job.

What to Expect from a Computer-Assisted Job Interview

A computer-assisted job interview proceeds in much the same way traditional job interviews do, except your interviewer is a large piece of expensive machinery. You get called for an interview, schedule a mutually convenient time to meet, come into the office, and meet with a human resources representative. However, instead of the traditional screening interview, you will be led to a computer workstation, where you will be given instructions on how to take the computer-assisted job interview. Most interview programs are intuitive and, providing you are computer-literate, easy to navigate. You are generally given a time limit, usually about thirty minutes, in which to finish the interview.

Expect to be asked about one hundred questions regarding your educational background, employment history, job skills, work ethic, and more. Here is an example of some questions you might expect from the ApView computer-assisted interview from Aspen Tree Software:

1. Are you currently employed?

   A. Yes
   B. No

2. Why did you leave your last job, or why do you want to leave your present job?

   A. I was dismissed
   B. I was laid off
   C. To take a better job
   D. Relocation
   E. To go to school
   F. I am not leaving my present job
   G. Other reason

3. How often do/did you experience conflict with your co-workers?

   A. Often
   B. Sometimes
   C. Rarely
   D. Never
   E. Cannot say

4. What kind of recommendation do you think your present or most recent supervisor would give you?

   A. Outstanding
   B. Above average
   C. Average
   D. Below average
   E. I don't know

5. Bob, on previous jobs were you able to develop new or better ways of doing the work assigned to you?

   A. Most of the time
   B. Usually
   C. Sometimes
   D. Seldom
   E. Never

In the past, most computerized job interviews consisted entirely of multiple choice or true/false questions, but now some computerized interview systems contain a number of questions that require more extended, written responses. Naturally, these types of answers are reviewed by a recruiter or hiring manager, not a computer. Most computer-assisted interviews are custom-made for each company or position. Generally, the interview is developed to address specific issues for a given position or family of positions. This eliminates the possibility that you will be asked questions that are irrelevant to the position for which you are applying.

You should answer the questions in a computer-assisted job interview just as you would in a traditional job interview. Don't exaggerate your skills and accomplishments. For instance, don't tell a computer you have five years' experience in retail if, in reality, you only have experience as a seasoned shopper. Remember, a computer-assisted interview is only the first step; if you get selected for a face-to-face interview, the interviewer will see from your application and resume that you were lying to the computer, which will virtually eliminate you from contention.

What's more, it's important to be more accurate with computerized interviews because, unlike their human counterparts, computers will immediately pick up on any inconsistencies in your responses. A human interviewer may be too distracted to pick up on any contradictions during an interview, but a computer is programmed to flag inconsistencies for the interviewer to discuss in your follow-up interview.

At the same time, don't be *too* honest to the computer. Several studies have shown that people are more honest with a computer because the computer is unbiased and not judgmental. People are likely to tell a computer facts about themselves that they would never dream of telling a human interviewer, especially in sensitive areas. However, before you bare your soul to a computer, remember that the computer will simply feed your answers to a very human interviewer as soon as the interview is over. In short, never tell a computer anything that you would not tell a real interviewer.

What the Computer Tells the Interviewer

Once you have completed the interview, the recruiter will explain to you the next steps in the interviewing process. Generally, the program will analyze your responses and present a summary to the recruiter. The recruiter will read the report and then decide whether you have the qualifications that would warrant a second interview. Among other things, the report summarizes basic background information, like education level and length of employment with your past or current company. **It will also highlight those questions where you had an abnormally long pause before responding.** This is done because several studies have shown that it takes longer to lie than to tell the truth. The report also flags inconsistencies and contradictions in your responses. For instance, some systems may have tricks worked in, so if you gave a certain response to a particular question or set of questions, the computer will flag those responses for the recruiter. Most programs will also provide the recruiter with a list of follow-up questions that is based on your answers to the computerized interview. For instance, in the sample questions listed earlier, the follow-up to question number five is, "Give me an example of something you developed on a previous job that enhanced a work assignment."

Some programs will also compare the results of your interview with a standardized employee profile that has been developed for a particular company. By comparing your answers with those of successful hires, the computer can predict—usually with measurable success—whether you will be a successful employee.

One important note: A computer never makes the final hiring decision. It simply presents a report to an individual recruiter, and it is up to this individual to analyze the data provided and determine whether or not to invite a candidate in for a second interview. So don't worry about your fate being in the hands of a machine; for better or worse, the final decision is still left up to a real person.

Why Employers Like Computer-Assisted Job Interviews

Aspen Tree Software, the makers of the ApView interview system, reports that employers like computer-assisted job interviews because they ensure that each candidate is thoroughly and— most importantly—impartially screened. With computer-assisted interviews, the information gathered is more accurate and reliable. What's more, advocates of these systems believe that the selectivity of the computer screens out borderline candidates who may have otherwise advanced, thus improving the overall quality of employees. One company reported a 33 percent lower turnover rate in the first six months of using a computer-assisted interview for the initial screening interview. Some other advantages of the computer-assisted job interview include:

- avoids traditional interviewing problems, such as forgetting to ask important questions or letting personal feelings interfere with the interview
- gathers more information about a candidate in one-third the time it would take a human interviewer
- information is more accurate—applicants are more likely to be honest with a computer
- hiring managers can focus on more important issues

Companies also often use computerized interviews for situations where accuracy and honesty are essential, such as exit interviews, in-house promotion interviews, or to measure employee morale and attitude. Since people are generally more honest to a computer, companies can get a more accurate reading of their employees.

How Computer-Assisted Job Interviews Can Help You

The previous section discussed why companies like using computer-assisted job interviews. This section will discuss why you should like taking computer-assisted job interviews.

By now you might believe that the computerized job interview is another step towards the depersonalization of the workplace by a corporate America that's increasingly beginning to resemble "Big

Brother." But you should be aware that the computerized job interview offers job hunters several important benefits.

The biggest benefit is probably the same reason you might balk at the prospect of sitting down for an interview with a computer: it's impersonal, unfeeling, and unsympathetic. Thus, with a computer, you are freed from the biases that, to some extent, every human interviewer possesses. A computer won't be judgmental or prejudiced—it won't have preconceptions based on your gender, race, height, weight, clothes, or voice. In short, computers are objective interviewers. A computer will never—consciously or subconsciously—allow personal feelings and biases to cloud its assessment of a candidate.

Computers are also less intimidating. A computer can't lead you to answer in a particular way, either verbally or through body language. Similarly, a computer won't react after you answer a question—no raised eyebrows, cringes, or even smiles. Since you aren't receiving any feedback, you can feel free to answer honestly, instead of giving an answer you think the interviewer wants to hear.

A computer-assisted job interview also helps to keep the playing field level. Often, a less qualified applicant will advance ahead of a more qualified applicant, solely because the less qualified applicant happens to have a stronger personality. However, with a computer-assisted interview, you can be assured that you are judged on your skills alone.

Finally, you can also be assured that the computer will be concentrating 100 percent on you and your interview. A computer won't be thinking about an overdue project, a critical meeting later in the day, or what it's going to have for lunch. What's more, you don't have to worry about encountering a computer that is simply having a bad day.

Of course, a computer-assisted job interview still has a few major shortcomings. First, some people say that the questions in these programs are biased against certain groups, especially women and minorities. Also, a computer is not always able to take into account certain special circumstances, such as a history of unemployment because of a disability or family obligations, and will thus provide a negative report to a recruiter. Finally, a computer is not, obviously, a person. A computer is not able to discern the intangibles that make us who we are—it cannot measure eagerness and enthusiasm, or alternatively, negativity and pessimism. So while a computer is generally more efficient than a person, it can never fully replace the human touch in the hiring process.

Computerized Applicant Screening by Telephone

Job interviews via the telephone are nothing new to job hunting. The telephone interview is often the first contact a job hunter has with a potential employer: A human resources person or hiring manager will call up a candidate, ask a few basic questions, and, if those questions are answered satisfactorily, invite the candidate in for a face-to-face interview.

A computerized telephone interview is really no different from a regular telephone interview. It's designed to get a better sense of a candidate's background to help determine suitability for a particular position. Aspen Tree Software and Pinkerton Security and Investigation Services are just two of the companies that create this type of telephone interview. With the ApView interview from Aspen Tree Software, an applicant calls a phone number and—using a touch-tone phone—answers some basic questions regarding his or her qualifications for a particular position. If the candidate meets the position's requirements, then the candidate can simply schedule, over the telephone, a more in-depth interview. Aspen Tree reports that this system is especially helpful to companies that are planning to hire workers in large numbers, such as for site openings or seasonal employment.

Pinkerton Security and Investigation Services designs computerized structured interviews for client companies. Offered as part of their pre-employment assessment services, the IntelliView

Structured Interview System is a 100-question interview about an applicant's employment background. These questions are of the yes/no variety, which makes it easier on the applicants because they have less information to remember before they respond. This system, which can be administered either over the telephone or on a computer, is generally not custom-made for a particular company or position, but rather, the industry in general. Each interview contains about 100 generic questions regarding a specific industry, such as retail, health care, child care, or work area, such as customer service. For instance, someone taking the child care interview may be asked if he or she likes to work in an orderly, quiet environment. If the candidate answers yes, then this person probably would not last long working in a daycare center.

Most of the advantages of the telephone interview are similar to those for the computer-assisted interview. They save a company time by efficiently screening out unqualified applicants, and can help improve the overall quality of employees. For instance, an unqualified applicant won't get by because he "sounded nice." For job applicants, the process is free from bias, so they can answer questions honestly and accurately. Furthermore, you don't have to worry about being put on hold while the interviewer tends to an urgent matter in the office.

The Internet Job Interview

This method of interviewing is quickly gaining popularity, especially for long-distance job hunting. For instance, say you're applying for a position with a company in Chicago, but you live in San Francisco. If you are hooked up online, you can simply complete a screening interview on your own home computer—instead of paying for an expensive flight and hotel room. Again, the process starts like any other: You are contacted for an initial screening interview, but instead of scheduling an initial telephone or face-to-face interview, you are provided with a password that gives you access to the company's in-house computer system. Once you log on, the process is essentially like that of a computer-assisted job interview. You are asked basic questions about your background and work experience, and the computer generates a report for the recruiter. Again, companies like this method because it's a big time-saver, but it is also beneficial to job hunters, since travel expenses for job interviews are usually paid for only the most high-level executives, or most highly sought college recruits.

Scenario-based Job Interviews

Like the name implies, scenario-based interviews involve more situational interviewing than the structured, computerized multiple choice interviews that were discussed in earlier sections. These types of systems are used to see how candidates will behave in simulated, real-life work situations. Learning Systems Sciences, a leader in this type of computerized interview, reports that their clientele consists primarily of banks and retail establishments, including many large department store chains. Like the structured, computerized job interviews, these interviews are most often used to screen candidates for entry-level positions that traditionally have high turnover rates. If candidates pass these simulations, they will be brought in for a face-to-face interview.

John King, vice-president of Learning Systems Sciences, reports that many companies prefer this type of interviewing because instead of simply asking someone, for instance, how they feel about customer service, the employer can actually see how a candidate will perform in tough situations. For instance, the computer screen might show an irate customer yelling about a product he bought that he believes is faulty, and the candidate must try to placate the customer.

Instead of simply keying in one of a set of preformulated answers, the computer actually records the voice of a candidate, thus allowing the recruiter to hear how the candidate handled the situation. Did the candidate remain calm and polite, or did the voice sound harried and rude? Candidates are usually graded on a decided-upon scale. For instance, a candidate might get extra points for apologizing to a customer, but could get points taken away if his or her voice didn't sound sincere.

Since these types of systems actually assess how well someone can read a particular situation and act appropriately, companies that use them report lower turnover rates than those that still use traditional methods. Like users of the computerized, structured job interviews, companies that use these systems also report an improvement in the overall quality of employees.

Of course, this type of scenario-based interview also helps candidates get a realistic idea of what to expect when they're on the job. For instance, many people say they like working with people, but that doesn't always include rude and unpleasant people. If someone is unable to handle a tough situation on a computer, chances are he or she wouldn't be able to handle one in real life. Of course, it's better to find this out before you actually accept a position and begin work. On the other hand, if you can pass this type of interview, then chances are you should be able to handle any situation that comes your way!

COMPUTERIZED ASSESSMENT TESTS

Assessment tests are nothing new to the world of job hunting. For years, job applicants have been asked to take all kinds of tests to evaluate their suitability for a job. The reasoning behind these tests is simple: hiring new employees is time-consuming and expensive. By carefully screening applicants with both structured, computer-assisted job interviews and computerized assessment tests, recruiters can greatly reduce the chances that a new hire will leave after only a few short months, and consequently, the time and expense of another candidate search will be avoided. This chapter will look at computerized assessment tests, such as skills, integrity, and personality tests, that you may be asked to take during your job search.

Employers generally use three main types of assessment tests: skills, integrity, and personality. The purposes of each of these tests are pretty basic: skills tests determine if you have the ability to do a particular job; integrity tests help determine whether you will be a trustworthy employee; and personality tests tell the interviewer if your disposition is suited for a particular position. Depending upon the nature of the position you are applying for, you may be asked to take one, two, or all three of these tests. Most positions require some type of skills test, for example a math test for accountants and a typing test for administrative assistants. Some computer programmers are even asked to write a short program as part of their pre-employment testing. If you are applying for a position where you'll be dealing with goods or money, you will probably be required to take an integrity test. **Personality or psychological tests can be used in virtually any situation, but are especially common if you are interviewing for a management position or one where you would be working with sensitive material.**

Pinkerton, the well-known security and investigation firm, stresses that prevention—by using pre-employment screening such as personality and integrity testing—is the best way to reduce or eliminate serious workplace issues such as theft, drug use, or even employee violence. To this end, Pinkerton has created a number of automated integrity, personality, and skills tests, including the Stanton Profile, the Stanton Survey, and the Adult Personality Survey. You can expect to take these or similar tests in companies where you would be consistently dealing with products, money, or other sensitive matters.

What to Expect from a Computerized Assessment Test

Computerized assessment tests are generally administered after the initial screening interview, while skills tests can often be part of the initial screening process. However, personality and integrity tests are usually given as one of the last steps of the interviewing process. If you are asked to take a computerized assessment test, your interviewer will likely lead you to a semi-private or private room with a computer. After you receive instructions on how to use the program, the test will be administered, usually within a specified time limit. Depending on the nature of the test, you may simply answer multiple choice or true/false questions, or you may transcribe written information into a specific computer program. Integrity and personality tests typically contain upwards of 100 questions. Most are of the multiple choice, yes/no, true/false, always/sometimes/never variety. Once your time is up, the computer will score your work, and, if applicable, compare your answers to a specified profile. The computer then generates a report for the interviewer to review. It should be made clear that the computer doesn't actually tell the employer whether someone should or should not be hired; it simply tells the recruiter how a candidate fits in relation to other candidates.

Computerized Skills Tests

Skills tests are the most straightforward types of computerized assessment tests. Basically, they measure your aptitude for performing a specific task or duty. Anyone who has done any temporary work will be familiar with many computerized skills tests. These tests simply determine your proficiency in various word processing, spreadsheet, and database programs. With these computerized programs, you are asked to do some basic exercises using the various applications, and you are tested on your accuracy. With some tests, especially those for word processing programs, you will have a certain amount of time to—for example—format and write a document. Then the computer will not only test your accuracy, but also how much you managed to accomplish in that time. Similarly, a spreadsheet test might judge you on how quickly and accurately you can enter data and perform different functions on the spreadsheet.

Again, computerized skills tests cover all fields. An accountant or engineer may be tested on their mathematical or logical reasoning skills. A computer programmer might need to write a few lines of code or debug a problematic program. Or you may be asked to take a test that measures reaction time, or that tests your memory. With computerized skills tests, anything is possible.

Computerized skills assessment tests are measured on your raw score. Your score is then measured against a median, or average score of everyone who has taken the test. For instance, if you scored a seventy-five, and the median score is sixty-eight, that will show the employer that you have above-average skills. Unfortunately, there's no real way to prepare for skills tests. The best you can do is prepare for the type of test, such as a typing or math test, that is likely to be administered during a job interview by brushing up on those skills.

Computerized Integrity Tests

Integrity tests, such as Pinkerton's Stanton Survey, are another type of computerized assessment test. Basically, these tests measure your honesty and morals. The Stanton Survey, for instance, is designed to measure the moral standard by which you live. By moral standard, this doesn't just mean whether someone is likely to embezzle company funds or steal from the cash register. An applicant's level of honesty and moral standard can also help determine whether someone is likely to be tardy, socialize excessively during work hours, leave early, take long lunches, "borrow" office equipment, and so forth.

Integrity tests allow employers to measure the reliability, work ethic, and trustworthiness of a candidate. These traits are all important indicators of a candidate's future performance. For instance, a recruiter might question the candidacy of an applicant who, on his integrity test, stated that it's all right to lie sometimes.

When taking an integrity test, try to avoid absolutes, like always or never. No one is likely to believe you if you say you have never in your whole life lied, or you have never gotten so much as a parking ticket. **However, the best advice we can give you is to not try to outwit the testmakers.** They have been at this far longer than you, and are more likely to try to trick you. Your best bet is to simply be honest and try not to incriminate yourself too much. After all, no one is perfect.

Computerized Personality Tests

Personality tests are the most complex of all computerized assessment tests. These are generally used to test a candidate's personal make-up to see if his or her personality is suited for a particular job. Tests such as Pinkerton's Adult Personality Survey measure specific personality traits such as work motivation, adaptability, and trustworthiness. The results of a personality test are then compared against a standard, or norm, group which has been developed from all who have previously taken the test. For instance, if you are applying for a position as an insurance underwriter, your scores will be measured against a norm group of successful underwriters.

Companies like personality tests because they allow companies to see if you will "fit in" with the company and the position. This is beneficial to both you and the employer, because if you are ultimately not happy with your job, it hurts both you and the company. The company has wasted time and money to train you only to have you quit in a few months, while you have wasted time in a job that ultimately didn't make you happy.

Another Pinkerton test is the Stanton Profile, a hybrid personality/skills test that measures general employability. This test measures your work preferences; your score is measured against the minimum requirements of a particular job. For instance, the test will ask you a question regarding your adaptability, a good trait for someone applying for a position as an administrative assistant, but not for someone working in a stockroom, since that person will likely be doing the same tasks day after day with little variation.

While preparing for skills and integrity tests is difficult, preparing for personality tests is nearly impossible. First of all, many people aren't sure if they should let their "true" selves answer questions, or if they should answer questions based on the kind of personality they think the company is looking for. Experts differ on the subject. Some suggest you use your work personality, while others say you should just be yourself. Still others suggest coming up with a "character" based on successful (and unsuccessful) friends and colleagues.

Our advice? While it's good to look at what traits have made others successful, you must first look at what's gotten you where you are. If you have spent any time in the work force, you should realize that your work personality differs from your personality outside of work. Therefore, it is best to use what you have learned in the workplace—what is and is not acceptable workplace behavior to answer the questions.

And as with the integrity tests, try to avoid using absolutes like "always" and "never." A large number of always and never answers might make it look like you are lying, or worse, be a signal of extreme behavior. **No one is perfect, and employers tend to stay away from extremists because for the most part, employers look for moderation in candidates. And moderation is, to employers, normal.**

CHAPTER FIFTEEN

JOB HUNTING AND CAREER MANAGEMENT SOFTWARE

J ob hunting software is yet another electronic advance that has helped take some of the mystery out of looking for a new job. Like most software products, job hunting programs have made the job hunting process easier than ever before. While these programs can't go out and find a job for you, they can help you create more polished, professional-quality resumes and cover letters, organize your contacts and job leads, and prepare you for job interviews. All of this can make you a more attractive candidate for any employer who looks for these characteristics—professionalism, organization, and preparation—in potential employees. What's more, many packages also include job hunting tips on everything from networking to what you should wear to a job interview. Some programs even have sections on assessing your career, which helps you figure out what jobs are best suited for you based on your personality and experience, as well as your likes and dislikes.

Whether or not you decide to invest in one of these software packages will largely depend on your individual needs. Do you simply want to write your resume, or do you want help with other areas of job hunting, such as finding out what questions you are likely to be asked during a job interview? And if you simply want to create a new resume, what kind of word processing software do you own? Many word processing programs already contain several different styles of resumes on templates. If you only want to change the format of your existing resume—or you want to create a new resume and you already have a good idea of what to say and how to say it—then you can probably make do with what's already available on your word processing software.

If, on the other hand, you want to write a brand-new resume, but you're not sure where to begin, job hunting software can help. The software can walk you through each step of the resume writing process, and provide you with features such as prewritten phrases or samples on which to base your resume. Similarly, resume writing software allows you to create customized cover letters or other business correspondence with ease. Most resume writing programs include many of the same features commonly found in word processing software, such as a spell-checker, thesaurus, mail merge, and envelope printing. Some also have a feature that automatically condenses a resume onto a single page if it spills over to a second page.

Another advantage of resume writing software is the flexibility it offers. For instance, you can easily try out different formats to see which is most appropriate for your resume—usually with a simple click of a button on a toolbar. Or, you can create multiple resumes with various formats or objectives tailored for use with different companies or job openings. For instance, you could have one resume focusing on one set of skills and another emphasizing other experiences or skills.

However, the best part of job hunting software is the fact that these programs are far more than just glorified word processors. Most programs include a contact manager, a section on job interviewing, general job hunting advice, as well as other special features, such as a database of potential employers. The contact manager is often the most basic part of the software—it is essentially a database where you can enter information on contacts, job leads, potential employers, or other notes that could be helpful to discuss in a job interview. Most also come with a calendar function that allows you to schedule and keep track of events such as phone calls made, letters sent out, and job interviews.

The sections on job interviewing are often the most impressive part of the software. Most of these products come in CD-ROM versions, and the multimedia capabilities of that medium really bring these sections to life. You can actually see and hear interview questions, and listen to sample answers and tips on how to answer the questions. The packages feature advice from top experts in the job hunting and career development field. These experts give you the answers to dozens—and in some cases, hundreds—of questions you may encounter in a job interview. You also learn why each question is asked, and get advice on the do's and don'ts of responding to the questions. Depending on the program, you can also listen to expert advice on writing resumes and cover letters, or on the job hunt in general.

Again, not every job hunter needs all of the features found in these products. For instance, if you are by nature very organized and a good record keeper, then you probably don't need another source to manage your job hunt. Also, the sample interview questions and answers discussed in these job hunting packages are not much different than those found in the leading books on job interviewing. Similarly, you can find most of the same general job hunting advice given within the pages of any of the dozens of books on job hunting that can be found at your local bookstore. At the same time, this type of software can be invaluable to someone who simply doesn't know where to begin his search, or whose job search is in need of a jump-start. In particular, the sections on resumes and cover letters can help revive a tired old resume, and the nature of the multimedia CD-ROM makes the job hunting tips and interviewing advice more lively and engaging.

When looking at job hunting software packages, you'll notice that most products have the same basic components—resume writing capabilities, a multimedia section on interviewing, and a contact management program. Also, there's not a large price differential between products. However, some products emphasize one area more than another, such as resumes or interviewing, while others offer special features, like employer databases or access to the Internet. Unfortunately, as Macintosh owners are well aware, there is usually less of a selection to choose from when it comes to buying software—or any other computer accessories—for a Macintosh, and job hunting software is no different. However, while most software is available only for Windows, many of the leading resume software packages, including ResumeMaker Deluxe CD and The Perfect Resume, also come in versions for the Macintosh.

It's worth noting that software companies frequently release new and updated versions of their products. Therefore, while the features described on the following pages are accurate at the time of this writing, there can be no assurances that these will be the features available by the time you read this. Similarly, retail prices may vary slightly according to individual stores or region, and prices are subject to change by the manufacturer. That said, here are a few examples to get you started in creating the resume of your dreams:

Adams JobBank™ FastResume™ Suite

System Requirements: 486 or higher PC-compatible computer; Windows 3.1 or higher, including Windows 95; 4 MB RAM (8 MB recommended); 10 MB free hard disk space; double speed CD-ROM drive; sound card; mouse; modem (optional). Includes CD-ROM and 3.5" floppy "light" version.
Manufacturer's Price: $39.95
Adams Media Corporation, 800-USA-JOBS

Calling itself the "total job search package," the CD-ROM version of the best-selling *JobBank* series of books contains a database of more than 22,000 employer profiles and more than 3,500 executive search firms and employment agencies, as well as tips on writing resumes and interviewing for jobs. Information provided in most listings includes the name and address of the contact person for professional hiring, description of the organization, common professional positions, educational backgrounds usually sought, and benefits. You can easily target potential employers by searching the database according to company name, state, industry, or job title. The program also allows you to automatically create resumes and cover letters using FastResume and FastLetter, or you can customize one of the 1,200 samples. Using FastResume, you can also insert prewritten action phrases into your resume, and with FastLetter, use ready-made paragraphs in your job correspondence. Choose between letters designed for responding to classified ads, networking, and many other types. A contact manager helps you organize your job search by allowing you to track contacts and job leads, and schedule interviews. You also get expert advice on how to handle job interviews. Prepare for an interview by watching and listening to 100 common interview questions, and reviewing sample answers and advice on how to answer particular questions, including tips on how to handle salary negotiation. FastResume Suite helps you develop a personalized interview strategy, and what *you* should ask during the interview. FastResume Suite also provides everything you need to connect to the Internet and access the CareerCity Web site (http://www.careercity.com). There you can post your resume free of charge, check over 125,000 job listings, and send your resume via email to employers.

PFS: Resume Pro™

System Requirements: 486sx/25 or higher PC-compatible computer; Windows 3.1 and MS-DOS 5.0 or higher or Windows 95; 4 MB RAM (8 MB recommended for Windows 3.1, required if using Windows 95); 6 MB free hard disk space (9 MB for full installation); double speed CD-ROM drive; 8-bit sound card (16-bit recommended); SVGA graphic card and monitor; speakers or headphones. Retail Price: $49.95
The Learning Company (formerly SoftKey), 800-227-5609
This powerful job hunting software provides assistance with writing resumes and cover letters, preparing for interviews, researching potential employers, and managing contacts. The resume section has more than fifty sample resumes, covering ten different types of career situations, including business, recent graduates, and military or technical background. The "Resume Counselor" offers guidance in writing your resume, including tips on what information to include in each section of your resume. Recognizing the fact that many resumes are now scanned electronically before they're looked at by human resources professionals, Resume Pro includes a glossary of field-specific keywords that you can use in your resume. The software also has fifty sample cover letters to customize, as well as a list of "power words" to help you write original cover letters and other job-related correspondence. And if you have a modem, you can email or fax your resumes and cover letters to employers directly from your computer. The Job Search Manager allows you to keep track of all jobhunting activities, including a database for contact and other relevant information, as well as monthly and weekly calendars to help you plan interviews and other important events. Finally, the Multimedia Career Counselor offers you tips for every stage in your job hunt, including where to find job openings, writing your resume, and the job interview itself. The Career Counselor asks you 100 common interview questions, and provides you with sample answers and advice on how to answer the questions. The package also includes KeyLink® Silver, a database that contains contact information for over 8,500 companies. Also, the software provides you with access to the Internet and all the valuable job search resources available there.

The Perfect Resume™

System Requirements for Windows: 386/33 or faster PC-compatible computer; MS-DOS 3.3 or higher (5.0 recommended), Windows 3.1 or higher; 4 MB RAM available (Windows 95 requires 486/33 and 8 MB RAM); 4 MB free hard disk space; double speed CD-ROM drive; VGA or SVGA monitor; sound card; mouse. (Also available in 3.5" floppy version.)
Macintosh: Macintosh LC or higher; System 7.0 or higher; 4 MB RAM; 1 MB free hard disk space; double speed CD-ROM drive; 256 colors; mouse.
Retail Price: $49.95
Davidson & Associates, 800-545-7677

With advice from career development expert Tom Jackson, The Perfect Resume is a leader in the resume software market. It tells you everything you need to know about writing professional-looking resumes and cover letters, managing your job search, and handling job interviews. With Resume Builder, you can choose between chronological, functional, or targeted resume formats. It also includes a "Resume Hall of Fame," that contains over 100 sample resumes, as well as over 200 job titles to consider when creating your "target job description." You can also listen to expert advice on what to include in a particular section by simply clicking on that section. The Resume Express feature is a "brainstorming" session designed to let you write your resume in just one sitting. You simply answer questions about your experience, skills, and accomplishments, and the program automatically formats a resume for you. The Power Letters feature includes five different types of prewritten letters, including cover letters and follow-up/thank-you letters; you simply fill in the blanks with your own personal information. The Job Search Manager helps you keep track of your contacts, including names, addresses, and phone numbers. You can maintain phone logs, and there's also a place to enter notes from your job interviews. In the video section of the CD-ROM, Tom Jackson answers many of the most frequently asked questions regarding resumes, cover letters, and interviewing, including how to handle salary negotiation, whether or not to reveal that you were fired or laid off, and how to answer inappropriate questions. You can also find general job hunting advice on a number of topics, including goal setting, time management, and building a support system during your job hunt.

ResumeMaker™ Deluxe CD

**System Requirements: 386-Based 33MHz PC-compatible
or higher; Windows 3.1, Windows for Workgroups 3.11,
or Windows 95; 8 MB RAM, double speed CD-ROM
drive, sound card; 256 colors VGA adapter or higher;
speakers or headphones; mouse
Retail Price: $39.95
Individual Software, 800-331-3313**

ResumeMaker Deluxe CD is more than just resume writing
software; it's a complete guide to career planning and job
hunting. Guided Resumes and Cover Letters take you through
each step of the resume writing process to create
professional-looking resumes and cover letters. In the resume
section, you can choose from chronological, functional, or
focused formats. From there, you simply fill in the appropriate
information for each section. The focused resume option gives
you suggestions for writing a resume tailored for different
fields and situations, including technical, publishing, or recent
college graduates. The guided cover letter includes prewritten
paragraphs for each of four types of letters; again, you simply
fill in the blanks with your personal information. The "Winning
Edge" workshop includes tips on conducting your job hunt and
advice on how to use the latest job hunting technologies, such
as the Internet and resume databases. It also includes expert
advice on preparing a resume, interviewing, networking, and
career planning. Finally, the virtual interview section tells you
what questions you are likely to be asked in an interview,
along with sample answers and the "rationale" behind each
question and answer. The program also tells you what
questions you should ask in an interview, as well as what
questions you might be asked that are illegal. But the software
encourages people to plan a career, not simply get a job. The
software also includes a detailed Career Planner, a program
designed to help you find your ideal career. By answering
dozens of questions in each of three areas—work values and
environment, experience and interests, and abilities—the
program creates a personalized profile of your work
preferences. Based on your profile, the program generates a
"Personal Career List" of possible careers. And since this
system is not always perfect, you can continually modify your
answers to come up with a revised list of potential careers.

WinWay® Resume 4.0

**System Requirements: 386 PC-compatible or higher;
Windows 3.1 or Windows 95; 4 MB memory; 2.5 MB free
hard disk space; double speed CD-ROM drive or faster;
sound card. (3.5" disk version requires only 2 MB
memory, and does not require CD-ROM drive or
sound card.)**
Retail Price: $39.95
WinWay, 800-4-WINWAY

This comprehensive resume and job hunting software package
contains sections on creating resumes and cover letters,
managing contacts, and job interviews. The resume and cover
letter sections include more than 300 samples that cover
thirteen fields and more than 300 different job titles. The
resumes also cover fourteen different career situations,
including military personnel entering civilian life and frequent job
changers. A special feature of the resume and cover letter
sections is the AutoWriter function. For resumes, you can
either fill in your personal information for the resume to format,
or insert prewritten phrases into your resume. Similarly,
AutoWriter will supply you with prewritten paragraphs for a
number of different types of letters, including ad response,
networking, or interview follow-up letters. The Contact
Manager has fields for name, company name, and notes, as well
as additional space for more detailed information about the
company, such as annual sales revenue or history. The interview
section contains questions, answers, and advice in twenty-five
different areas. It even includes sections on how to answer
stressful or "off the wall" questions. What's more, the program
lets you skip around so you can look only at the area of
questioning you're interested in. The program includes some
additional features, including the *Dictionary of Occupational
Titles*, which contains detailed descriptions of thousands of job
titles in virtually every field, a Salary and Benefits Guide, and job
hunting strategies to follow before, during, and after the
interview.

The software includes both a CD-ROM and a 3.5"
diskette. While the diskette does not have the video and audio
capabilities of the CD-ROM, the contents are virtually the same,
except the diskette does not include the text of the *Dictionary of
Occupational Titles*.

GLOSSARY
OF
TERMS

ASCII: An abbreviation for American Standard Code for Information Interchange. It is the most basic code for written documents (such as resumes or letters) that all computers understand. ASCII files contain no special formatting, like italics or boldface. It was invented to enable different types of computers to communicate with each other. It's often referred to as DOS text or plain text.

Access: The ability to connect to a service or resource and receive information. Accessing certain services may require special software (as with commerical online services) or registration (as with Bulletin Board Systems).

Address: The combination of letters and/or numbers that enables you to reach another computer or user online. People with online/Internet accounts have email addresses where they receive their email. A fictional example of an address is, **yourname@computer.com**. On the Internet, the address is also called a URL.

BPS: BPS stands for bits per second, and it is the measurement of how quickly a modem can send and receive information via telephone lines. The slower your BPS, the longer it takes to receive information online, and the higher your phone and connect time charges. At the time of this writing, 28,800 or 33,600 BPS modems are the standard, but modem speeds are constantly increasing; 56,600 BPS modems are becoming more and more commonplace.

Baud: The scientific unit of measurement for data transmission speed. Usually measured as one bit per second. Not to be confused with BPS, which is the correct term for measuring modem speeds.

Bookmark: To store a site's Web page address, thereby eliminating the need to type in a URL every time you want to return to a particular site. This feature is found on most Web browsers.

Bulletin Board System: Commonly abbreviated as BBS, a Bulletin Board System is like a mini-online service, catering to communities or to particular interests. Basically, it's a computer set up with special software, a modem, and one or more phone lines which users access through a telephone line and communications software. It's an easy way for users to meet, exchange information, and find computer files and software. Many BBSs also offer their users some form of Internet access.

Click: To select an element, either some text or an image that appears on the computer screen, usually by pressing on the mouse button (once or twice, depending on the application) and cause another action to happen. For instance, on the Web, if you click once on underlined words, you will be transported to another document, file, or directory on the Web.

Clients: Special programs that retrieve information from other computers and computer networks, called "servers."

Commercial online service: A service that charges a fee for access to its online resources that were developed especially for the use of its subscribers. These services usually charge extra for access to particular services, such as databases or newspapers. The most popular commercial online services include America Online, CompuServe, The Microsoft Network, and Prodigy.

Communications software: The software that enables you to use your modem. Communications software controls the exchange of information between your modem and a remote modem.

Computer-assisted job interview: A job interview administered by a computer. It's designed to take the place of the traditional screening interview, and usually consists of multiple choice and true/false questions about a candidate's employment history and background.

Computerized assessment tests: Tests administered by a computer that help determine job fit. Computerized assessment tests usually fall into one of three categories: skills, personality, or integrity.

Cyberspace: A general term often used when referring to the Internet and other online services. It's also used when discussing computers in general. The word originated in William Gibson's novel *Neuromancer*.

Database: A large, organized collection of information that's stored electronically. A database's carefully constructed design enables users to search for and locate specific information—such as job listings in a particular field or location—quickly and easily.

Discussion group: An electronic meeting place for people with shared interests to chat, discuss ideas and issues, and exchange information through the posting and reading of messages. It's the general term used when referring to Usenet newsgroups, mailing lists, or special interest groups on commercial online services.

Download: To transfer data (such as files) from another computer to your own.

Electronic resume: A traditional resume that's stripped of most of its formatting so that it can be easily read and searched by a computer. An electronic resume is necessary in order to take advantage of electronic resume databases.

Email: Electronic mail. Email is a standard service that comes with most communications software, Internet connections, and commercial online services. It allows you to send and receive messages through your computer.

FAQ: Frequently asked questions. Compilation of questions (along with their answers) that are most commonly asked. Posted by most newsgroups, mailing lists, special interest groups, and other online services for the benefit of new or inexperienced users.

Forum: A specific name for special interest groups or discussion groups found on CompuServe, America Online, and Delphi, where participants can post and read messages regarding specific topics.

Freeware: Public domain software files that are available to users free of charge.

Gopher: A menu-based system that easily allows users to explore all areas of the Internet, usually with the help of a Gopher search engine, such as Jughead or Veronica. Gopher is often called the grandparent technology to the Web because of its easy-to-use menus, but recently, the growth of Gopherspace has stalled due to the rapid development of the World Wide Web.

HTML: Hypertext markup language, the text formatting language that makes use of hypertext and is used to write documents on the World Wide Web.

Home page: Home pages are usually maintained by companies, organizations, the government, educational institutions, and even individuals. The home page is also referred to as the first page of a Web site, where you can find, for example, the main menu of options.

Hypertext: Hypertext enables users to jump from one page to another to access information, such as text, graphics, or music, through predefined links. It's the concept upon which the World Wide Web is based.

Internet: The global network of computers that transmits information via telephone lines, enabling computers from all over the world to communicate with each other. It's used by many different organizations, such as educational, commercial, and government institutions, to convey news, entertainment, and other information to users worldwide. It's also the general term used when referring to Gopher, Telnet, Usenet, and the World Wide Web.

Jobline: A telephone line maintained by a particular company or organization for the purpose of announcing job openings. Especially popular among large corporations or other organizations that hire large numbers of workers, either regularly or on a seasonable basis.

Jughead: The smaller of the two main search engines for Gopher, the other being Veronica.

Keyword: A word or short phrase that is used to search a database of documents or files. When filed, documents, such as resumes, are indexed using a particular set of words that refer to key concepts within that document. When you perform a keyword search, the computer searches all documents and files within a particular database (or databases) for matches between the keyword and one of the indexed words.

Link: Created using hypertext, links are what connect you to a different site on the World Wide Web. The new connection may be with a different Web page or simply a file or subdirectory within a large site or down the same page. Links are most often represented by underlined words, though some may be presented as graphics.

Log in: Often "log on." To connect with a remote computer or computer network, such as a commercial online service or BBS.

Mailing list: Also known as list serve. A type of discussion group found on the Internet, in which users send and receive messages through email.

Meta-list: A "list of lists" found on the World Wide Web with links to Web sites and other Internet resources on a particular subject, such as job hunting. These lists are good time-savers since they generally include a short description or review of the site or service, so you won't waste time visiting irrelevant or low-quality sites. Plus, to access a particular site, you only need to click on the site name.

Modem: From MOdulator/DEModulator. A communication device that converts data from computers into sound that is transmittable via a telephone line, thereby allowing remote computers to communicate with each other through ordinary phone lines.

Multimedia: The joint use of several different forms of media, such as text, sound, graphics, and video in a single application, such as a Web page or CD-ROM.

Netiquette: The established set of manners used when participating in Usenet newsgroups and other online discussion groups. It's important to be familiar with the netiquette of a particular newsgroup before jumping into the discussion. Created from combining the words "network" or "Internet," and "etiquette."

Network: Computers that are physically connected, usually through hardware, to facilitate the sharing of information. There are two basic kinds of networks: Local Area Networks (LANs), which are relatively close together, in the same office, for instance; and Wide Area Networks (WANs) in which the computers are scattered across cities, states, or countries. Technically, the Internet is considered a Wide Area Network.

Newsgroup: The name of online discussion groups found in Usenet. These electronic message boards are by far the most popular type of discussion group, with more than four million regular users.

Online: To be linked via modem to another computer or computer network. To say that you're "online" generally means you are connected to a Bulletin Board System, the Internet, or a commercial service like CompuServe.

Post: Post, or posting, is used as both a noun and verb. As a noun, a post is what you may find and read online, such as job listings or a message in a newsgroup. As a verb, post is when you send a message or a document (like a resume) to a BBS, newsgroup, or special interest group.

Protocol: The set of rules that determine how different computers exchange information. For instance, the documents in the Web address **http://www.yahoo.com** must be retrieved using hypertext ("http" stands for hypertext transfer protocol).

Roundtable: The specific name for the electronic discussion group found on GEnie.

Search engine: An information or database retrieval tool that enables users to quickly and easily search the vast amounts of information found on the World Wide Web (some may also search Usenet). Two examples of search engines are Excite and AltaVista.

Server: A main computer or computer network that relays information when "asked" by special software called "clients."

Shareware: Software files that are available free to users for a limited time only, called an "evaluation" period. After the evaluation period, you must pay in order to use the software.

Site: A specific place on a commercial online service or the Internet (including the World Wide Web) where users can find information.

Special interest group: The type of discussion groups found on commercial online services. Includes bulletin boards, forums, and roundtables.

Telnet: A way of connecting to a remote computer or network over the Internet. You navigate Telnet by using command line prompts. It's also a *type* of Internet site that you may connect to. For example, you can Telnet directly to a Telnet site, or Telnet to a Gopher server.

Thread: A string of related messages on the same topic found in Usenet newsgroups and other discussion groups. It contains both original posts and replies to those posts.

URL: Short for Uniform Resource Locator. It's the uniquely identifiable address for any Web site—such as a file, directory, or other computer—on the World Wide Web. For instance, **http://www.whitehouse.gov** is the URL for the office of the President of the United States.

Upload: To transfer data (such as files) from your own computer to another computer.

Usenet: Abbreviation of User's Network. This is a vast, international network of more than 20,000 different online discussion groups on practically every topic imaginable. Usenet is only one part of the Internet, and was created specifically to allow users to exchange news and other information.

Veronica: The largest search engine for Gopher. Acronym for "Very Easy Rodent-Oriented Netwide Index to Computerized Archives."

Web browser: Software, such as Netscape Navigator, that enables users to navigate the World Wide Web. It "reads" the hypertext documents on the Web, including text, intricate layouts, and graphics, and presents them to the end users.

World Wide Web: The part of the Internet that uses hypertext links and graphics to convey all kinds of information—news, entertainment, and more. The hypertext links enable users to easily jump between different documents and files, thus making exploring the Internet both simple and fun. Commonly referred to as the Web.

INDEX

-A-

"A Beginner's Guide to HTML," 73

ABI/Inform (business periodical database), 219

Academe This Week/Chronicle of Higher Education (WWW job listing), 141

Academic Physician and Scientist (Gopher job listing), 190

Academic Position Network (Gopher job listing), 191

Accountants Forum (CompuServe SIG), 254

Adams JobBank FastResume Suite employer database on CD-ROM, 212
software, 19, 285

Adult Personality Survey (assessment test), 276, 279

Advertising/Marketing Professionals (Delphi SIG), 257

Alaska, joblines in, 203

Alta Vista (WWW search engine), 26

American Big Business Directory (employer database on CD-ROM), 212

American Business Information/American Yellow Pages (AOL employer database), 231

American Manufacturer's Directory (employer database on CD-ROM), 213

American Standard Code for Information Interchange (ASCII), 53

American Yellow Pages. See American Business Information/American Yellow Pages (AOL employer database)

America Online (AOL), 20-21, 89-90
and Gopher, 188
job listings on, 96-100
online company research on, 231-232

special interest groups on, 251-253

America's Employers (WWW employer database), 226

America's Job Bank (WWW job listing), 142

AMIA/MedSIG (CompuServe SIG), 254

Anonymity, and job hunting. See Confidentiality

AOL. See America Online

AOL Classifieds/Employment Ad Boards, 96

Applicant tracking systems, 18, 47-50
advantages of, 48-49
disadvantages of, 49-50

ApView computer-assisted interview sample questions from, 265-266
by telephone, 271

Architecture and Building Forum (CompuServe SIG), 254

Arizona, joblines in, 203

ARPANET. See Internet

ArtJob (Gopher job listing), 192

ASCII (American Standard Code for Information Interchange), 53

Aspen Tree Software, and computer-assisted job interviews, 264, 271

Assessment tests, computer-assisted, 19-20, 275-280

Atlanta (GA) resume posting, on Usenet newsgroups, 62

-B-

BBSs. See Bulletin Board Systems

Best Jobs USA (WWW job listing), 143

Big Book (WWW employer database), 227

The BBS Corner (list of BBSs), 198

Bookmarking sites, on World Wide Web, 138

Books and Writing (Prodigy SIG), 258
BostonSearch (WWW job listing), 144
Broadcast Professionals Forum
    (CompuServe SIG), 254
Bulletin Board Systems (BBSs), 20,
    197–200
    job listings on, 199–200
Business America on CD-ROM
    (employer database), 213
Business and Company ProFile (business
    periodical database), 220
Business Database Plus (CompuServe
    employer database), 232
Business Dateline Ondisc, UMI (business
    periodical database), 220
Business periodical databases, 209,
    218–221
    list of, 219–221
The Business Resource Directory
    (GEnie), 106

-C-

California, joblines in, 203
Canada job listings, on Usenet
    newsgroups, 129
Canadian Resume Centre (WWW), and
    resume posting, 66
CareerBuilder (WWW job listing), 145
Career Center (AOL), 97
CareerCity (WWW)
    employer database, 227
    job listing, 146
    resume database, 63
Career Connections (Prodigy), 110
Career Exposure (WWW job listing),
    147
Career Forum (Microsoft Network SIG),
    258
CareerMagazine (WWW)
    employer database, 228
    job listing, 148
Career management software, 281–289
CareerMart (WWW)
    job listing, 149
    resume database, 64
CareerMosaic (WWW)
    employer database, 228
    job listing, 150
    resume database, 64
Career objective, in electronic resume,
    31–32
CareerPath (WWW job listing), 151
Career Profiles Database (GEnie), 107

Career Resource Center (WWW), 139,
    239
Careers (Prodigy SIG), 258
Career Search-Integrated Resource
    System (employer database on CD-
    ROM), 213–214
Career Shop (WWW)
    job listing, 152
    resume database, 64
CareerSite (WWW)
    job listing, 153
    resume database, 64
CareerWEB (WWW job listing), 154
CD-ROMs, and video/multimedia
    resumes, 82–83
Characters per line, in plain text files, 55
Chicago Tribune Classifieds (AOL), 98
Chronicle of Higher Education. See
    Academe This Week/Chronicle of
    Higher Education (WWW job listing)
College Grad Job Hunter (WWW job
    listing), 155
Colorado, joblines in, 203
Colorado Jobs Online (WWW), and
    resume posting, 66–67
Commercial online services, 20–21,
    23–25
    and company research, 231–237
    definition of, 87
    fees for using, 92–93
    and Internet access, 92–93
    job listings on, 96–114
    and keywords, 94
    and resume posting, 60–61
    special interests groups on, 250–259
    and Usenet newsgroup access, 117
Companies International (employer
    database on CD-ROM), 214
Company directories. See Electronic
    employer databases
Company joblines. See Joblines
Company Profiles (WWW employer
    database), 228
CompuServe, 20–21, 90
    job listings on, 101–103
    online company research on,
        232–237
    special interest groups on, 253–256
CompuServe Classifieds, 101
Computer-assisted job interviews. See
    Job interviews, computer-assisted
Computer Consultants (CompuServe
    SIG), 254

Computerized assessment tests. See Assessment tests, computer-assisted
Computer literacy, importance of, 16–18, 56
Computers, for electronic job hunting, 24
Confidentiality
    and electronic employment databases, 42
    and online resume databases, 57–58
Contact manager, in job hunting software, 282–283
Contract Employment Weekly (WWW job listing), 156
Cool Works (WWW job listing), 157
Corporate Affiliations (CompuServe employer database), 233
CorpTech Directory (employer database on CD-ROM), 214–215
cors (electronic employment database), 43
Country codes, in URLs, 137
Court Reporters Forum (CompuServe SIG), 254
Cover letter, electronic
    with electronic resume, 34–35, 71
    example of, 36
    keywords in, 35

-D-
Databases. See Electronic employer databases; Online resume databases
Delaware, joblines in, 204
Delphi, 21, 87, 89, 92
    job listings on, 104–105
    special interest groups on, 256–257
Desktop Publishing Forum (CompuServe SIG), 255
Direct Internet connection, 24–25, 93
Disclosure SEC (CompuServe employer database), 234
Discussion threads, in Usenet newsgroups, 116–117
District of Columbia, joblines in, 204
DORS (electronic employment database), 43
Dr. Job (GEnie), 108
Dun & Bradstreet Online (CompuServe employer database), 235–236
Dun's Electronic Business Directory (CompuServe employer database), 234

Dun's Million Dollar Disc Plus (employer database on CD-ROM), 215

-E-
EDGAR Database of Corporate Information (WWW employer database), 229
Education (Prodigy SIG), 259
Education Forum (CompuServe SIG), 255
Electronic cover letter. See Cover letter, electronic
Electronic employer databases, 19, 209–221
    list of, 212–218
    and relocation, 211
    search options on, 211
Electronic employment databases, 39–47
    and confidentiality, 42
    and professional profiles, 40
    and relocation, 41
Electronic job hunting
    equipment needed for, 23–25
    reasons for utilizing, 16–18
Electronic Job Matching (electronic employment database), 44
"Electronic portfolios," 77. See also Multimedia resumes
Electronic resumes, 18, 29–50
    career objective in, 31–32
    circulating, 39–50
    content of, 30–32
    conversion to plain text file, 53–55
    cover letter with, 34–35, 71
    emailing directly to company, 69–71
    example of, 37–38
    follow-up after emailing, 70
    format of, 33–34
    keywords in, 30–31
    keyword summary in, 31
    multimedia. See Multimedia resumes
    posting online, 51–83. See also Online resume databases
    subject line, 59, 64
    video. See Video resumes
    and word processing programs, 54
Electronic revolution, 16
Email
    and electronic resumes, 69–71
    and traditional "snail mail," 69
Employer databases. See Electronic employer databases
E-Span Career Management Forum (CompuServe), 103

E-Span Job Listings (CompuServe), 102
E-Span's Interactive Employment
  Network (WWW)
    employer database, 229
    job listing, 158
    resume database, 65
Excite (WWW search engine), 26
  as company URL directory, 239
Exec-PC (BBS job listing), 199
Extreme Resume Drop (WWW), and
  resume posting, 67

-F-

Federal Government Employment
  Opportunities (AOL), 99
Federal Job Opportunities Board
    BBS job listing, 199
    Telnet job listing, 194
FedWorld Federal Job Announcement
  Search (WWW job listing), 159
Follow-up, of emailed resumes, 71
4.0 Resumes and Job Listings (WWW
  resume posting), 67
4WORK (WWW job listing), 160

-G-

Gateway Virginia (Prodigy), 111
General Business Forum (Delphi), 104
GEnie, 21, 87, 92
    job listings on, 106–109
GEnie Research and Reference Services,
  109
Georgia, joblines in, 204
Get a Job (WWW job listing), 161
Gopher, 21–22, 187–192
    and America Online, 188
    job listings on, 190–192
    search engines, 188–189

-H-

Harris Complete (employer database on
  CD-ROM), 215
Health Professionals Network (AOL
  SIG), 251-252
HEART: Career Connection (WWW job
  listing), 162
HEART's Career Connection (Telnet job
  listing), 195
Help Wanted (WWW job listing), 163
Help Wanted USA (AOL), 100
HispanData (electronic employment
  database), 44
Home page, on World Wide Web
  for companies, 224, 237–241

for job hunters, 71–73
Hoover's Business Resources (AOL
  employer database), 232
Hoover's Handbook on CD-ROM
  (employer database), 19, 216
Hot Jobs (WWW job listing), 164
Houston (TX) resume posting, on
  Usenet newsgroups, 62
HTML (Hypertext markup language)
    and electronic resumes, 51–52, 71–73
    sites for learning, 73
Hypertext, 134
Hypertext markup language. See HTML
Hypertext transfer protocol, and URL,
  136

-I-

Idaho, joblines in, 204
Illinois, joblines in, 204
Illinois resume posting, on Usenet
  newsgroups, 62
Indiana, joblines in, 204
Information Management Forum
  (CompuServe SIG), 255
In-house resume database, 39. See also
  Applicant tracking systems
The Institute of Electrical and Electronics
  Engineers (WWW job listing), 165
Integrity tests, computerized, 278
Intellimatch (WWW job listing), 166
    resume database, 65
IntelliView Structured Interview System,
  271-272
International job listings, on Usenet
  newsgroups, 129–131
Internet, 21, 25
Internet access, and commercial online
  services, 92–93
The Internet Access Company (TIAC),
  73
The Internet Job Locator (WWW)
    job listing, 167
    resume database, 67
Interviews. See Job interviews
InvesText (CompuServe employer
  database), 236–237
Investext on InfoTrac (business
  periodical database), 221
ISCA (Information Systems Consultants
  Association) BBS (job listing), 199

-J-

JobBank USA (WWW)
    job listing, 168

resume database, 65
Job Center Employment Services
  (WWW), and resume posting, 68
The Job Complex (Delphi), 105
JobExchange (WWW job listing), 169
Job hotlines. See Joblines
JobHunt (WWW), 139
  company URL directory, 239
Job hunting software, 19, 281–289
  and job interviews, 269
Job interviews
  computer-assisted, 19-20, 263–274
    benefits for employers, 268–269
    benefits for job-hunters, 269–271
    by Internet, 272–273
    scenario-based, 273–274
    by telephone, 271–272
  and job hunting software, 283–84
  researching company before,
    218–219
  structured, 264
Joblines, 19, 201–205
  selected listings by state, 203–205
Job listings
  America Online, 96–100
  bulletin board systems, 199–200
  commercial online services, 96–114
  CompuServe, 101–105
  Delphi, 104–105
  GEnie, 106–109
  Gopher, 190–192
  Prodigy, 110–114
  Telnet, 194–195
  Usenet newsgroups, 119–131
  World Wide Web, 137–185
    on companies' home pages,
    237–241
JobNet (WWW job listing), 170
JobServe (WWW job listing), 171
JobSource (WWW job listing), 172
Job Trak (WWW job listing), 173
JobWeb (WWW)
  employer database, 229
  job listing, 174
Journalism Forum (CompuServe SIG),
  255
Jughead (Gopher search engine), 22,
  188–189

-K-
Keywords
  on commercial online services, 94
  in electronic cover letter, 35
  in electronic resume, 30–31

Keyword search, on WWW, 139
Keyword summary
  in electronic resume, 31
  in HTML resume, 72

-L-
The Law Forum (Delphi SIG), 257
Learning Systems Sciences, and scenario-
  based interviews, 273
Legal Exchange (Prodigy SIG), 259
Legal Information Network (AOL SIG),
  252
Lexis-Nexis (WWW employer database),
  229–230
Liszt: The Mailing List Directory, 250
"Lurking" online, 245–246

-M-
MacEAST (BBS job listing), 199
Macintosh computers, 24, 284
Magellan (WWW search engine), 139
  as company URL directory, 239–240
Mailing lists
  networking on, 243–245, 249–250
  online directories of, 250
Martindale-Hubbell Law Directory
  (employer database on CD-ROM),
  216–217
Massachusetts, joblines in, 204
MBA Interim Solutions (WWW job
  listing), 175
Medical resume posting, on Usenet
  newsgroups, 62
MedSearch America (WWW)
  job listing, 176
  resume database, 68
Meta-lists, on World Wide Web, 139,
  226, 239–241
The Microsoft Network, 20–21, 87,
  90–91
  special interest groups on, 257–258
Microsoft Word, 54
Mid-Atlantic USA job listings, on Usenet
  newsgroups, 121–123
Midwest USA job listings, on Usenet
  newsgroups, 124
Modems, 24
The Monster Board (WWW)
  employer database, 230
  job listing, 177
  resume database, 65
Moody's Company Data (employer
  database), 217
Multimedia resumes, 18–19, 75–83

appropriate uses for, 76–78
and CD-ROMs, 82
creating, 80–82
disadvantages of, 82–83
format of, 76

-N-

The National Job Hotline Directory, 203
The National Job Line Directory, 203
National (USA) job listings, on Usenet
newsgroups, 127–129
National Resume Bank (electronic
employment database), 44–45
NationJob Network (WWW job listing),
178
"Netiquette" online, 245–247
Netscape Navigator, 73
and Usenet newsgroups, 117–118
Netscape News, 118
Networking online, 243–259
on America Online, 251–253
benefits of, 244
on CompuServe, 253–256
on Delphi, 256–257
on mailing lists, 249–250
on Prodigy, 258–259
on special interest groups (SIGs),
250–259
on Usenet newsgroups, 247–249
New Mexico resume posting, on Usenet
newsgroups, 62
Newsday (Prodigy), 112
Newsgroups. See Usenet
newsgroups
New York City resume posting, on
Usenet newsgroups, 62
New York, joblines in, 204
NL Professionals Forum (CompuServe
SIG), 255
Northeast USA job listings, on Usenet
newsgroups, 121–123
Notepad (text editor)
and plain text files, 54–56
Nursing Network Forum (Delphi SIG),
257

-O-

Online business periodicals, 224
The Online Career Center (WWW)
job listing, 179
resume database, 52, 65–66
Online Classifieds (Prodigy), 113
Online company research, 223–241
advantages of, 225

on America Online, 231–232
on commercial online services,
231–237
on CompuServe, 232–237
on World Wide Web, 226–231
Online networking. See Networking
online
Online Opportunities (BBS job listing),
200
Online resume databases, 51–52,
56–58
and confidentiality, 57–58
downloading from, 59
fees for using, 60
and HTML resumes, 71–73
posting resumes to, 51, 58–59
and relocation, 57
and subject line, 59
on World Wide Web, 226–231
Online strategies, 25–26
Open Market's Commercial Sites Index
(company URL directory), 240
OPM Mainstreet (BBS job listing), 199

-P, Q-

Paper resume, importance of, 52–53
Passport Access (WWW job listing), 180
PC-compatible computers, 24
Periodicals. See Business periodical
databases
Personality tests, computerized,
275–277
PFS: Resume Pro (software), 286
Philadelphia (PA) resume posting, on
Usenet newsgroups, 63
Photo Professionals (CompuServe SIG),
255
Pittsburgh (PA) resume posting, on
Usenet newsgroups, 62
Placement Services-Sites for Job
Seekers and Employers (WWW),
139, 226
P.L.A.C.E.S. Forum (AOL SIG), 252
Plain text file
characters per line in, 55
conversion of resume to, 53–55
Portland (OR) resume posting, on
Usenet newsgroups, 62
Prodigy, 20–21, 87, 91
job listings on, 110–114
special interest groups on,
258–259
Professional profile, on electronic
employment database, 41

ProPublishing Forum (CompuServe SIG), 256
Protocol, of URL, 136
Publicly Accessible Mailing Lists (directory), 250
Public Relations and Marketing Forum (CompuServe SIG), 256

-R-

Relocation, 41
   and electronic employer databases, 211
   and electronic employment databases, 41
   and online resume databases, 57
   and Usenet newsgroups, 119
Researching potential employers. See Business periodical databases; Electronic employer databases; Online company research
Resume
   electronic. See Electronic resume
   paper, importance of, 52–53
Resume Bank (WWW), and resume posting, 64
ResumeCM (WWW), and resume posting, 64
ResumeMaker Deluxe CD (software), 284, 288
Resume posting. See also Online resume databases
   on targeted WWW sites, 66–69
   on World Wide Web, 63–66
Resume Pro Database (WWW), and resume posting, 65
Resumes-on-Computer (electronic employment database), 45
Resume writing software, 282
Retail JobNet (WWW job listing), 181
Rhode Island, joblines in, 204
The Riley Guide (WWW), 139

-S-

San Francisco (CA) resume posting, on Usenet newsgroups, 62
Search engines
   for company URLs, 238–241
   on World Wide Web, 26, 139
Seattle (WA) resume posting, on Usenet newsgroups, 63
Server, of URL, 136–137
   codes for, 136–137
Shawn's Internet Resume Center (WWW), and resume posting, 68

SIGs. See Special interest groups
SkillSearch (electronic employment database), 45–46
Skills tests, computerized, 277–278
Software. See Career management software; Job hunting software; Resume writing software
South Dakota, joblines in, 205
Southeast USA job listings, on Usenet newsgroups, 123
Southwest USA job listings, on Usenet newsgroups, 125–127
Special interest groups (SIGs), 250–259
   on America Online, 251–253
   on CompuServe, 253–256
   on Delphi, 256–257
   networking on, 243–244, 250–259
   on Prodigy, 258–259
Standard & Poor's Register (employer database on CD-ROM), 217–218
Stanton Profile assessment test, 276, 279
Stanton Survey assessment test, 276, 278
Strategies, online, 25–26
Student Center (WWW employer database), 230–231

-T-

Talent Bank. See Worldwide Resume/Talent Bank (online resume database)
Tampa Bay Online (Prodigy), 114
The Teacher's Lounge (AOL SIG), 252
Technology revolution, 16
Telephone interviews, 271–272
Television broadcasting, and video resumes, 77
Telnet, 21–22, 187, 193–195
   job listings on, 193–195
Text editor, 54–56
Text file. See Plain text file
The Perfect Resume (software), 287
Thomas Register Online (CompuServe employer database), 237
Threads, discussion, in Usenet newsgroups, 115–117
TIAC. See The Internet Access Company
TOPJobs (WWW job listing), 182
Traders Connection (BBS job listing), 200
Travel Professionals Forum (CompuServe SIG), 256

-U-

Uniform Resource Locators. *See* URLs
University ProNet (electronic
    employment database),46–47
URLs (Uniform Resource Locators), 72
    for companies, directories of,
        238–241
    protocol of, 136
    server of, 136–137
    structure of, 136–137
USA Jobs (WWW job listing), 183
Usenet newsgroups, 21, 22, 115–131
    and commercial online services,
        115, 117
    discussion threads in, 116–117
    hierarchies in, 115–116
    and Internet carriers, 117
    job listings on, 119–131
    and money-making "scams," 121
    networking on, 243–249
    for new users, 117–119
    posting resumes in, 61–63
    protocol of, 61
    and relocation, 119
    structure of, 115–117
    for test messages, 118

-V-

Vermont, joblines in, 205
Veronica (Gopher search engine), 21,
    188–189
Video resumes, 18–19, 76–83
    appropriate use of, 76–78
    and CD-ROMs, 82
    creating, 78–80
    disadvantages of, 82–83
    format of, 76
    and television broadcasting, 77
Virginia, joblines in, 205
Virtual Job Fair (WWW job listing), 184

-W-

Washington DC, joblines in. *See* District
    of Columbia, joblines in
Washington (state), joblines in, 205

Watercooler (Microsoft Network SIG),
    258
Web. *See* World Wide Web
Web browsers, 73
Web page. *See* Home page, on World
    Wide Web
Web site. *See* Home page, on World
    Wide Web
West USA job listings, on Usenet
    newsgroups, 125–127
WinWay Resume 4.0 (software),19, 289
Wisconsin, joblines in, 205
Women's Network (AOL SIG), 252
WordPerfect, 53–54
Word processing programs, and
    electronic resumes, 53–54
Worldwide Resume/Talent Bank
    (AOL/Internet resume database), 52,
    61
World Wide Web, 21, 22, 133–185
    drawbacks of, 134–135
    history of, 134
    home pages on, 71–73, 224,
        237–241
    job listings on, 137–185
    meta-lists on, 139, 226, 238–241
    and online company research,
        223–231
    and online resume databases, 57–59
    resume posting on, 63–66
        to targeted sites, 66–69
    speed of, 135
The World Wide Web Resume Bank,
    68–69
The Writers Club (AOL SIG), 252–253
Writer's Forum (CompuServe SIG), 256
WWW. *See* World Wide Web

-X, Y, Z-

Yahoo! (WWW)
    as company URL directory,
        240–241
    job listing, 185
    as search engine, 26, 139
Your Business (Prodigy SIG), 259